Spirit in The Wind

By

Rev. C.E. Guldenschuh

Spirit in The Wind by Rev. C.E. Guldenschuh

DEDICATION FOR SPIRIT IN THE WIND

To properly thank everyone who made this book possible would take at least another book, not to mention, more words than I could ever gather in one place at one time. Having said that, I want to pay tribute to:

The memory of my father, Charles Paul Guldenschuh, who taught me to not only survive but how to really live, how to move forward with purpose and that a real man is tough enough to be tender. You will always be the high water mark of what a man is supposed to be.

My mother, Ella Jean Guldenschuh, who taught me to find the positive even in the midst of the negative, to see through the eyes of compassion and the strength of unconditional love. Proverbs 31 was written with you in mind.

My wife, Sarah Criswell Guldenschuh, who supports even my wildest ideas with a heartfelt "go for it", stands by me no matter what and keeps me getting up and going for another day. I told you that life as you knew it would never be the same!

Last but not least, I dedicate this book to all those out there that have been there, done that and lived to tell the tale. We are survivors, you and I. Know that you are not alone out there.

BECAUSE

To my father on Christmas 1987

Because you brought me into this world and

 Taught me the best that you knew how

Because you disciplined me when I was wrong

Because you praised me when I did well

Because you taught me to respect God

Because you taught me to achieve

Because when I was down you picked me up

Because when I was dying you taught me to live

Because every time I wanted to tell you that

I love you

I did not know how

A TENDER CARESS

Sometimes, when I become heavy in heart, and

my mind refuses to believe in tomorrow,

I feel the loneliness known only to the single star which

faintly sparkles in a never-ending void.

I feel as if I am alone,

alone through eternity.

My spirit falls as a windless sail

begging for even the slightest breeze to touch me.

Longing for even the tiniest wisp of hope.

At times such as these, even the tenderest of caresses

can mean so much.

BIRD SONG

Listen to the sunrise.

Feel the velvety glow of pastels,

Crimson and gold

They glide across the silky sky.

Close your eyes. Hear the bird song,

Wind chimes whispering in the wind.

The dew on the grass is like a city of

A thousand, silvery lights.

Like diamonds in white sand dunes.

BIRTH, DEATH, AND RESURRECTION OF AN UNTAMED SPIRIT

THE INSTANT OF THOUGHT...

THE WHISPER OF HOPE...

THE NEED OF LOVE...

THE DECISION OF PURPOSE...

THE STRUGGLE TO ATTAIN...

A thought, an idea. Does reality exist, or are we just a thought?

Are we a fragment of shattered chaos, or are we the many atoms of an

energy. Some say we are the physical extensions of a magnificent being. But,

does this source exist in time, or space, or is it just an idea.

What defines time and space? Time is but a passing mist. If one is idle, then

he has already lost that moment. If one uses an instant, then it has been

created and recorded forever. The shell is gone, but the spirit remains.

To man, earth's journey about the sun may seem unending, but when he realizes

that his galaxy revolves around another, his concept of time is transposed.

And what is space? Is it the location of an object, or of a mind.

Cannot man's mind exist both within his head and at the same time

within a different world? Some believe that space is the creation of

a thought. But, then you may say why be concerned with time and space.

In essence, is that not the same as asking why be concerned with our own existence?

The whisper of hope. If we did not hope, then we would only exist.

We would not grow or learn. We would be unable to accept or be accepted.

We would be as the stars in the heavens, just there.

We need hope. It is hope which causes us to reach for that which

we do not have, whether it exists in reality or not. If it lives in our minds

as a thought, then it is real to us.

The need of love. We need love. We need to be loved.

It is love which strengthens our spirit. Without strength we would

wither and die. We would be as the leaves of a tree in autumn.

They wither, die, and once again become one with the earth. It is love

which spurs hope onward. Love can be many things. What is love for

another person? It could, in essence, be a form of envy. A person who loves

someone sees traits in that person, which he wishes he possessed. He is

drawn as a magnet to steel. It could also be enjoyment of an object or

an action. Love will always be one thing, of the spirit.

The decision of purpose. Every living being has some decision of purpose,

no matter how menial it may seem. The decision to think. The decision to be.

The decision to survive. There cannot be a purpose without first having

decision.

The struggle to attain. The final goal. It may take a lifetime, or

maybe an eternity. Time is irrelevant. The struggle is first spiritual, then

physical. One sets a goal in his mind, then uses his body as a tool to acquire. Which is more rewarding, spiritual treasures which

last an eternity, or material gains which fade away with the body?

CAN YOU HEAR ME   (A SONG)

Can you hear me when I call to you in the singing of the birds.

Can you hear the message that is hiding in these words.

My heart is straining with the thought of all the joy that you have brought

To fill the empty shadows of my life.

It is hard to live in wonder. It is hard to live in fear,

When people that I care for leave me in my tears.

I want so much to love someone and hope that they won't turn to run

I feel no one hears me when I call.

CAPTIVE TO NONE

Fly, sweet scent of spring,

upon the wings of April winds.

The eagle, soaring to the heights of the skies,

in regal glory shines.

His strength is seen as he glides past the sun,

dipping his wing to turn.

His gentleness is far surpassed by his graceful,

feathery furls.

He is honor and justice. He is king of the skies.

He is challenged by all, but,

captive to none, he remains.

COME SIT WITH ME

Come inside lonely stranger

Come inside and sit with me

Tell me of your journey

Did you find the road to set you free

HOPE

To view the sunrise with awe is a spiritual feeling,

knowing that it is a rebirth of a new day.

A rebirth of our life, giving us the chance to

reclaim those lost moments and resurrect them as

the spirit of hope,

perchance we would strive to make each coming moment meaningful.

IF ONLY YOU KNEW

If only you knew the birds that sing their special songs for you.

If only you knew the beauty in the sparkle of the dew.

If only you saw the flowers and the sun that shines for you.

If only you felt the waters that forever flow for you.

If you could only open up your heart to let the emptiness inside

be filled with warmth and tenderness by ones you have denied.

If only you could perceive, alas, not the past you have been through.

Then, you could see the yearning love that I have kept for you.

If only you knew.

INDIAN SUNSET

Red sun departs from turquoise sky

Silver moon begins to shine

The eagle soon will take his rest

The owl leaves his cozy nest

The night is warm the air is still

Your raven hair glistens like silk

Your eyes of blue look deep within

My inner thoughts of you, Maghian

Tomorrow brings another day

Again, my love, I go away

The time has come you need not cry

My love for you will never die

Now I must go I pray these words

Will warm your heart throughout the years

I WILL BE THERE

My friend, I have come again. You always seem to listen.

You roar back answers to my questions.

Your beloved angels sing melodies of comfort

as they frolic in the sun.

Yes, my friend, I will always come to ease your weary soul.

When the sun no longer smiles upon you, I will be there,

my friend.

LIFE

Life, as days go by, sees many things.

The sun coming and going, chasing the moon,

resting high at noon.

Life is a magical occurrence.

It is the soul in a body's flask.

Of its origin we often ask.

From where does life's soul come?

If man is created from dust, then

Is life born of trust?

Who can say what life is?

If life is found in breath, then

Is the absence of breath death?

LISTEN

May God look upon you and smile.

His love will warm your heart and

His voice shall be beautiful music unto your ears.

All you have to do is listen.

LONELY DREAMER

Clouds drift lazily overhead like thoughts

in the mind of a lonely dreamer.

They are carefree, and linger not.

they are here, then gone.

The majestic ocean stretches far as the eye can see.

The gull feels secure because of the lullaby.

White sands tell their own story by

grasses waving in the breeze.

Driftwood lies forgotten by the sea

like a child's scattered toys.

When the lonely dreamer sees all this,

he is not really lonely, after all.

LOVE

Love is the sun so bright and warm chasing away the storm.

Love is the tree with all it's freedom warmed by the sun.

Love is the shade given by the tree so cool and free.

Love is for people, especially for two.

Love is you.

MAN BY THE ROAD

I've traveled far, day by day. The road's become my friend.

Many people share my life, the stories never end.

I won't begin to tell them all, but there is one I can't forget,

a young man crossed my path one day, a stronger man I've never met.

Alone I've been for many years. Myself, I thought I knew.

He shared with me a story that I'd like to share with you.

I met him in the country, I had napped beneath a tree.

When I awoke, there he sat, quiet as a leaf.

We looked each other eye to eye and we spoke not a word.

The world seemed to freeze as ice, our thoughts were not disturbed.

He began to speak and I to hear, his voice was clear as rain.

His eyes became as distant stars as he to me did say:

"Think, before you answer me, and tell me truthfully,

Look deep within yourself, tell me who you see.

You've spent your life upon the road. You've traveled day by day.

Do you know the road you walk; do you know the price you pay?

The road you walk you cannot see with eyes nor feel with feet.

The price you pay is not in coin, which quickly can deplete.

The road you walk is life itself, but is your life your own?

Are the stories you can tell me yours, or to someone else belong?

Can you tell me of yourself, or people whom you've met?

Can you tell me what you've done, or why the sun does set?

Can you tell me why the grass does grow, or why the bird does sing?

Can you tell me why the flowers bloom, or why the bells do ring?

The price you pay is in your loss of not living your own life.

Don't get me wrong, because all along there was struggle, pain, and strife.

Look down this road that is yet to come.

Tell me what you see. Will you travel to the end, or

until your heart does plead to rest your weary bones beneath the

cloudy skies above to await the crossing overhead of

the peace-bringing dove?

Look upon this roadway that you have traveled up till now.

This roadway tells the story of your life, your loves, your crowns.

So, you see, you have lived your life in living day to day.

All the wealth that you have earned is worth the price you paid.

Now rest, you sir, beneath this tree. Set aside your tools.

I shall carry on your journey as I walk on in your shoes."

MELANCHOLY DAYS

Ah, these days I hold with deepest feeling.

Cool and breezy, they come most welcome.

Memories return on each wisp of loneliness

being sifted through the leaves.

Ah, these melancholy days.

Sadness touches my heart like arrows.

The sun hides its warmth from me behind a mask of dingy skies.

I am reminded of a walk down an empty Country Lane,

believing myself to be alone in the world.

No one seems to share my woes or pains.

Ah, these melancholy days, I love them so.

The more loneliness I feel, the more I realize that

I am not unfeeling for those I hold dear.

MISTY LADY (A SONG)

She sails alone on an empty sea

The sun shines only briefly

All her life she waits for me

She's my Misty Lady

The sea begins to toss and turn

Truth and respect she hopes to earn

She waits for her sails to unfurl

As she sails ever onward

The tempest now is close at hand

There is no sight of land

She's unsure of her destiny, but

Hope drives her onward

The eye of God is watching her

She finds comfort in His word

She fears not the uncharted course

His guiding hand will lead her

The storm recedes and the calm returns

She hears the song from the wings of the birds

Her faith has brought her through danger's grasp

As she sails ever onward

From beaten bow to battered stern

To the warmth of the harbor she returns

Her spirit is strengthened, her faith renewed

Now she'll rest till the morning

Now the ropes moan no more and the oak does not weep

She makes her final voyage to the endless deep

Sailing into the glorious mist

Full masted in all of her glory

PEACE

Listen to the bullfrogs croak.

Like a symphony of tubas they endlessly sing.

Ah, the cool shade is so inviting as you

watch the ripples in the pool.

PROTECTIVE BOUGHS

These being the words within my heart,

I wish to bequeath, when I depart

all the memories which I hold,

the warm times and the cold,

the good times and the bad,

the new and the old.

To the trees I leave my paper and pen.

Oh, all the poetry that I've written

beneath it's protective boughs.

Through the ages, my thoughts will browse.

To the sun I leave the flowers and trees,

the morning dew and vines born of my mind.

To the world I leave my love for all to remember that

I was born of the sunshine and the streams.

SCENT ON THE WIND

Softer than the sunrise is her skin.

Warmer than the afternoon is her love.

She is a dove flying high to be seen by all she loves.

She is fragrant, light as a flower in the middle of a field.

SONGS OF THE WATERFALL

PART ONE-THE JOURNEY

Peace, peace and serenity fall upon me,

covering me with a blanket of warmth.

No thoughts.

A mist of melancholy enshrouds me.

No thoughts, only emotions.

My spirit takes leave.

As I pass above the tall trees' reaches I feel their strain,

as if they wish to bring to an end my aerial journey.

I sense my spirit traversing great distances and times,

to a place I have never before been.

Again, I feel peace as I rest beneath trees,

beside cool waters,

I have no fear, for

this forest is at peace with my heart.

PART TWO-THE SONGS

As I rest, I see the waters,

a stream of many lives and tales.

The stream is in no hurry, for

it has passed this way before, and

will again.

As the waters pass over the falls,

I first hear the sounds of many trickles,

like soft whispering.

I strain to listen, for

there is a message for only my spirit to hear.

The waters now sound as soft, sweet music,

music such as I have never before felt.

The music surrounds me,

fills me with love.

It causes me to feel as a vapor on the wind.

I look upon the foot of the falls.

I see many stones,

stones which the waters have nurtured for time unknown.

The waters' tender caresses have

polished these stones into jewels.

The value of these stones lies in the

understanding of their cause and being.

These jewels shine as many colored lights

throwing their radiant rainbow firelight for my eyes to feel.

they appear to me as jewels set into a crown.

PART THREE-THE TALES

I lie backward against the tree with closed eyes

that I might feel, with my spirit,

the entire beauty of my private world.

I hear with my ears, an orchestra of sounds,

each sound separate, but also one with the others.

I bathe in this magical music as if I were floating on a cloud.

Sounds surround me, birdsong,

the chatter of squirrels and chipmunks,

even the gentle sound of the butterfly's fluttering wings.

As I listen, these wonderful sounds become one with my spirit.

Understanding fills the very depths of my soul.

I hear and feel the tales of my private, sylvan dream

as remembered by the many creatures

who have endured the bounds of time

as if their sole purpose was to await my arrival.

My spirit reaches now to those very few who

hear these words and understand the songs of the waterfalls, as

I have understood.

STRONGER

The higher and harder mountain a man climbs,

the stronger in spirit and love he becomes.

TAKE ME (A SONG)

Take me, take me down to the woods,

down to the water where the sun sets the mood.

Take me, take me, because I want to go.

I love the feeling of freedom, so.

When I was a younger lad,

I remember the good times we had,

roaming aimless through the fields,

lie under trees and kick up our heels.

I remember in the spring of the year,

we would watch as the green leaves appeared.

In the summer we'd run to the creek,

prop our cane poles up on skinny, forked sticks.

In the autumn we watched the trees

as they changed colors and flashed in the breeze.

In the winter we'd walk through the snow

chasing a rabbit, or maybe a doe.

Take me, take me down to the woods,

down to the water where the sun sets the mood.

Take me, take me because I want to go.

I love the feeling of freedom, so.

Take me, take me because I want to go.

I love the freedom of feeling so.

I FEEL THE THUNDER 7/11/82

Today has found me sitting, wondering, where am I ?

In time past, this was my home. Since my return,

I have slowly noticed the change.

Plastic people with eyes that do not see, but

seem to stare into the distance,

looking through me as though I were a window, but,

now, the curtain drawn, they see me no more.

The skies appear to me,

now as a river, muddied by the constant shifting and turmoil.

The day is not calm, but saddening.

The thunder rolls, but I hear it not.

I have been deafened to its call.

I feel the thunder as it were a thousand curses to life.

It's heaviness falls upon my chest,

weakening my heart with each new wave.

Life, here, has been trying, being, and hoping for good.

As I sift my battered emotions to the winds, and

they are carried to the trees,

I find no rest, although, I feel the thunder, as if it were

the roar of the mighty ocean.

Thunder, please tell me of truth, and change, and rebirth.

I must learn, I must grow, I must die,

only to be reborn in a new light,

with new emotions.

I stare into the darkness of many blind eyes.

There is only one window that I see,

having a lighted taper, which shares its warmth and hope.

As the heavens darken from my view,

I shall remember this one candle which

shines in a sea of dimming thoughts. Now,

I feel the thunder,

the light is you.

BARREN TREES (A SONG)

I gaze upon my world and see reflected to me,

The image of the soul I have received.

Barren trees, barren trees, standing alone against the sky.

So am I, so am I.

Memories of days gone by, no more to try.

I can see there is a reason to cry.

Barren trees, barren trees, standing alone against the sky.

Against the sky.

Once there was life here on every twig and bough.

There stands now only memories of how

Barren trees, barren trees stand alone against the sky.

So am I, so am I.

So am I, so am I.

SO AM I, SO AM I.

A BUTTERFLY'S WINGS 7/12/82

I sat among wild flowers mixed among weeds.

Shadowed by mighty branches of massive trees.

Birds were singing passively as they busied with their lives.

Bees were carrying nectar to make honey in their hives.

Everything around me seemed so very serene,

God sent me a butterfly, it's voice soft as a dream.

At first I puzzled at this gift and could not understand.

Then the butterfly, light as wind, had lit upon my hand.

Sitting quietly, I did not move. I uttered not a word.

The beauty of this creature, I dared not to disturb.

In my heart was whispered, "This is my spirit I send you.

Cherish this with all your soul before this day is through."

Of secrets, hopes, and dreams, and fears,

I learned, and touched, and grew.

Within my heart I know these things are everlasting true.

that voice, again, spoke to me, and brought to me this thought,

"See Me not with your eyes, but hear Me with your heart.

I rest My spirit within your hands. I know I must not flee, although, as a butterfly, I am sturdy as a tree.

Hurt not this most tender of gifts I bear, throw not into the sky.

Touch with love, and hope, and care, if need, allow to cry."

I cannot relate in words alone, the feelings that I touched

by being trusted by a friend, and trusted with so much.

My life is given to those who need someone to hear and feel.

To those from whom I learn and grow, on bent knee I kneel.

To those who learn from me, I wish to never empty be. For,

I myself, have received the gift of

the trust of a butterfly's wings.

GIFTS ARE FOR SHARING 7/12/82

In my thoughts I have browsed, often wondering of my purpose.

I have questioned myself in times past, where have I met this one, or

that one ?

What have they shared with me ? Now,

what have I to offer ?

Gifts, I have received.

Should they be kept in secret closets ?

Gifts, are they for sharing?

I live to share with others,

an offering of my life, in hopes that,

through my suffering they may be strengthened.

Yes, gifts are for sharing.

My prayer is that my words and music shall not be buried with me, but

that I shall live on, through them,

to help yet one more.

Gifts are for sharing.

UNFINISHED BECAUSE OF A SILENT TEAR 7/12/82

Such faith, as I have never before known,

has entered into my life.

She sang songs to me which no one had ever before heard.

She shared with me a trust she knew I would keep

MY DAYS ARE EMPTY WITHOUT YOU 7/12/82

Though I have no rights, no claims, no guarantees, and

I should not ask, but

my days are empty without you.

Your voice, soft as a flower, rings within my memory as

the music of your heart.

Your eyes, to me, are candles in the dark.

No rights, no claims, no guarantees, but

my days are empty without you.

TOAST AND TEA 7/13/82

I watched the sunrise this morning.

It made me think of you.

Thank you for your morning.

CAN I TOUCH THE STRINGS 7/14/82 5:03 AM

At this moment, she is a memory, a memory until we are together next.

As I think about her, I can almost see her.

I'll close my eyes. yes, I can see her now.

I can remember, oh so many different colors In her eyes.

I could tell, no, feel that she was troubled.

We were drawn together in a special way, such as a magnet is drawn to iron.

We felt that we each had something to share.

I remember, I asked her, once, about a question mark.

It was a start, which I was later to learn, of a conquest, or

maybe a sojourn, or maybe a final battle which,

win or lose,

had to come of time.

We both shared this same struggle.

We had to learn to trust completely, and

feel completely trusted by the other.

We set out on that long, hard climb, hoping and praying that

we would find our waterfalls.

Along that road, we made many stops.

We talked of butterfly wings, and life, and pains.

We hoped that by sharing we would learn, and grow, and

be stronger for the times to come.

She shared with me through words, and I through writing and music.

I learned about her through listening to her emotions, feelings, voice.

I hope that whatever I can share with her will help her toward her dreams.

I feel so inadequate in what I have to offer her.

She seems to need more than a lot of people are willing to give.

My prayer is that I can always give her what she asks of me.

I want, so much, to help her find her waterfall.

I remember on one stop, she trusted me with a teardrop,

which I shall preserve, for myself only,

along with my deepest, silent tears.

I was so touched by her that I have found

new springs for my rivers to flow.

I remember on another stop, I had taken a step closer to my dream.

I had trusted her,

I didn't have to, it just happened.

We talked of many times, memories, tomorrows.

She will always be a part of me,

in presence, in spirit.

HAD I CREATED WOMAN 7/14/82 6:30 pm

Had I created woman,

I would make her eyes with the sparkle of a million stars,

her skin as soft as the petal of a rose,

her voice as smooth and light as a birdsong.

I would not have molded her thoughts.

Her mind and heart are hers alone.

Had I created woman,

I would not have created her to be held on a pedestal, or

to be worshiped as an idol, but

to be held, dearly, near to my heart.

Had I created woman, she would be one of

my greatest gifts to all life.

A PUFF OF SMOKE 7/14/82 6:07 pm

Many times, lately, maybe not enough,

I think about tomorrows and dreams.

I wonder if I'll ever find mine, or

If I really want to.

Sometimes, I feel I can almost reach out,

touch my dreams, but

then they become like a puff of smoke, and

disappear into my pool of memories.

I wonder if one can really touch one's dreams?

Will they always be just that, dreams ?

If, one day, I find my waterfall, will I be complete ?

I feel there will always be an important part missing.

Where do I go from here,

when I have no more dreams ?

FOOTPRINTS IN THE SAND 7/14/82 dusk

Footprints in the sand.

Once, a reality, now only memories.

Memories to tell me that I have walked so far,

oh, so far.

Where do they start,

where do they end,

these footprints in the sand?

ICE CREAM 7/16/82 4:30 pm

I ate your ice cream this morning, and

I remembered all the snow-covered hills that we slid down on

sleds made from cardboard boxes, and

wishing you were there.

I remembered walking down the icy sidewalks,

watching our breath turn into steamy clouds then disappear, and

wishing you were there.

I remembered building a snowman, so fat,

they had to be fat, and

wishing you were there.

I JUST WANTED YOU TO KNOW 7/16/82 12:43 am

I have tried so many times to write this.

I can't seem to find words worthy of my emotions.

Understand, that this is the hardest, highest risk moment

which I have known.

I stand to possibly lose much of me, all of me, all of you.

I stand to possibly gain. my loss is meaningless when

compared to the loss I may bring to another.

I hope that you can read between the lines and

feel what I am feeling.

I don't want to change you.

I don't want you to change me.

I want us to grow.

I don't know if you understand me, or once you do,

whether you can accept or not these emotions bound within me.

My days are empty without you.

I don't feel I have the right to come to capture your time,

your presence.

I do want so much, to learn your total being, but

what makes me feel that I am worthy of your care?

Am I ?

I listen to you, I cling to your words, facial expressions,

tones in your voice.

My silence is telling you that I understand,

I care.

My silence is telling you that

there is something that I want to share with you, but

I am afraid.

Something, I want to blurt it out, but I can't.

I have tried, but was unable to let you know.

I want, so much, for you to see, but I am afraid.

Maybe I can bring myself to tell you.

Maybe I don't want to tell you.

I have given you a puzzle, but have kept one piece for myself.

I have drawn you an incomplete picture.

You can see me from one side, not from the other.

In order for you to understand, I must give you a key.

I stand before the gate of my waterfall.

The gate is locked and I have a choice.

My waterfall is complete, less one very essential part.

I now face a risk, a risk of importance I pray you will understand.

If I turn the key, it may be the wrong key.

If the gate remains locked, then I have lost everything that I am.

If the gate opens, then I will be complete.

I don't want to take that risk.

I would rather stand in anguish,

looking in at my waterfall, and not entering, than to

turn the key and find that it may not open.

The loss I cannot face.

The risk, I feel, is necessary to me.

I hope you can begin to see.

How can I come right out and tell you ?

How can I open this part of me to your eyes ?

I feel that I need to take that risk now.

Think about our thoughts last night.

My waterfall is here.

The key to the gate is here, but

am I worthy ?

Am I worthy to turn that key ?

I know in my heart that this key

would complete my picture puzzle, but

this key is not accessible to me.

I don't know how else to say this, except in plain words.

The key to my waterfall is you. But,

I can't have you completely.

I can't love you completely.

I have not said this to you, but I do trust you.

I trust you more than I trust myself. But,

can't you see, I've let myself get too close.

I have never before known anyone to care for me

as deeply as I feel you do.

I have never before known anyone to

understand me as deeply as I feel you do.

Can you see the risk I am taking ?

I risk losing everything that I am.

Can I bear that ? I want you to know how I feel.

I don't want to change you.

I don't want my feelings to cause you to run from me or to me.

I Just want you to know.

SO I COULD UNDERSTAND 7/16/82 5:42 am

To really know me, and for me to know myself,

I must relate, to you, a story.

My hope is that you will listen to my story, and

try to understand me.

Many years ago, more than I can remember,

I asked a prayer.

Knowing God would understand, I asked not for jewels,

not for money, not for gold nor diamonds, but

for understanding.

I asked that I be taught understanding through suffering.

I had seen many suffer and I had no words for them.

I was without understanding,

I was ashamed.

One year led into the next.

Time had continued it's hurried pace until, finally,

my questions had been answered.

I was stricken in the speed of a thought.

I suffered so that I could learn

to understand pain, anguish, and other treasured lessons.

I learned not to pity, but to care.

I learned not to shut out, but to share.

I learned not to die, but to live.

I learned not to take, but to give.

Suffering became as much a part of me as my heart,

keeping me alive, or

my emotions, helping me to grow.

I respect pain.

It teaches me many lessons in understanding.

My eyes have been returned their sight so that

I may see others' sufferings, and have words, and understanding.

I cherish people who share their suffering with me.

By hearing, feeling, understanding others,

I learn, I grow.

If I care too deeply, sometimes, let me know.

I don't want to chase you away.

I look to see others' sufferings,

to feel others' sufferings,

to have words, to understand,

to care, to not be ashamed.

when I understand,

I will have found God.

I CRIED 7/16/82 8:47 pm

I cried inside today.

I missed you.

I NEED YOU 7/16/82 9:03 am

I started to write this, but

then, I couldn't.

THE STORY OF DAVID 7/17/82 5:46 am

In memory of David Pepper, age 4

I wish you could have known him.

He was much younger than I, but

he brought to me a gift or, maybe he was a gift.

I only met him once, but

I seemed to have known him for a lifetime.

When I saw him, the other children did not share with him.

He was a loner.

He was flying paper airplanes to himself.

I joined him.

He didn't push me away.

He shared with me, for I, too, was a loner.

He felt that.

We lined the children up to take them across the lawn.

He took me by the hand because he had no father at home,

because I shared with him,

because, even though a child, he understood.

He touched me with a feeling,

bringing tears to my eyes.

He cried inside, too, but it was a happy cry,

He masked it with a smile.

I never saw him again.

When I had returned I was told that he had left us.

No gloomy sky can express the feelings and

emotions which were mine.

David, David, where have you gone ?

Can you hear me calling ?

I remember that walk on the lawn,

the day you took my hand.

David Pepper died of cancer.

I DON'T UNDERSTAND 7/17/82 3:22 pm

I think about things that you say, and I search myself for answers.

I tear open my soul for those answers, but still, I find none.

I ask myself, how can you feel that I have so much to give ?

I don't feel worthy of the gifts you offer.

I don't feel worthy.

I don't understand.

ECHOES 7/17/82 3:32 pm

Before I met you, I knew you.

I wanted to tell you,

if you want to talk, I want to listen.

SILENCE 7/17/82 3:40 pm

When I don't say anything,

I Just want you to know

I don't know how to say

what I want to say.

AGE 7/17/82 3:56 pm

We spoke of age, once.

I told her I was as young as a newborn baby, and

as old as time itself.

A WHOLE NEW WORLD 7/18/82 3:22 am

I went for a walk today, and I learned.

I saw ants running, seemingly madly,

like people in the city, and each one had a purpose.

I saw rocks, big ones, small ones, and I saw sand.

I learned there will always be one greater and one lesser than I.

I saw grass, like skyscrapers, and I was amazed.

I went for a walk today, I watched the ground,

I learned of a whole, new world.

I KNEW 7/18/82 4:56 am

I thought about you tonight, and I worried.

I knew you didn't feel well. I cared.

I wanted to be there.

I knew you were lonesome.

I was happy for you, and I smiled for you because

I knew you were strong

ALL THE RIGHT THINGS 7/18/82 11:49 pm

I wish I could say all the right things, right now, but

maybe nothing is the right thing to say.

I WANTED TO TELL YOU 7/19/82 6:12 am

Sometimes, I think about all the times I wanted to tell you that

I cherish the time we spend together. That

when I am silent, my heart cries for you. That

I sit on my doorstep each day,

knowing that you will spend part of your morning with me. That

sometimes, I Just want to embrace you, and

say thank you because you cared,

because you understood. That

I am happy when you are with me. That

I miss you when you are gone. That

I wish you could talk, and I could listen, but

time moves too fast. That

even though I don't say it,

thank you for being you. That

you have made me feel there is trust. That

I wish I could say I love you, but

I don't know how.

MAYBE 7/19/82 9:13 am

I don't want to say that you forced me,

I Just couldn't help myself.

Maybe it's because you share so much with me,

your time, your emotions, your care, your understanding.

Maybe it's because you go out of your way for me.

Maybe it's because you trust in me.

Maybe I don't feel worthy of such treasured gifts.

Maybe it's because you say so many things that

I want to say to you, but I don't know how.

Maybe it's because you fed me in the mid morning,

just because you cared.

I don't want to say you forced me, but

how can I do anything except

cherish you.

I LEARNED TODAY 7/19/82 9:35 pm

I learned a new experience today. another side of trust,

like the world was given to me.

The world of spiritual gifts, feelings, emotions.

I felt my heart in my hands.

The only world that existed was ours.

I felt so happy I cried inside.

I learned much of gentleness, caring, understanding through trust.

Though time erases many things,

I shall never forget that moment.

A DREAM 7/20/82 3:00 am

Last night was so very special.

I learned so many new lessons. I felt so many new emotions.

The best part was that we shared.

I learned how deeply I could care, how great my need,

gentleness, tears of happiness, all because of trust.

When we reached out and touched, it was not flesh,

it was trust. Pure trust.

I felt so full inside.

Every cell in by body came to life.

My sleeping spirit had awakened.

It pains me deeply that words are not nearly adequate

to express my emotions.

I felt so totally free.

I had unlocked another of the many shackles protecting the

many gates of my waterfall.

It was such a beautiful, new experience.

Our hearts seemed to beat as one.

I could feel, even in my hands.

Yes, I cried inside, into the very depths of my being.

They were tears of joy,

such joy that I did not want to lose that moment.

I have placed that moment, gently and tenderly,

into my treasure chest.

I placed it, passionately, among other jewels,

jewels such as a tile having the circle of life.

That tile will, one day, share with me the story of Mandy.

I patiently await.

There is a jewel of a gift, icy and smooth,

which was on the outside, a warm gesture.

On the inside it was a plea, please accept this because

I care, I understand, it is alright.

There was another jewel, that of a mid morning traveler.

It touches me too deeply at this time.

There are so many jewels, already.

Time passes slowly. These jewels are the

precious stones lying at the foot of my waterfall.

They are so beautiful. I treasure each one,

They mean so much to me.

I will always remember last night.

I will not allow time to wear it smooth.

I will keep it always as sharp and as clear forever.

I felt so happy inside. I was so touched that

my heart begged to explode,

my lungs tried desperately to finally rest.

I thought, if I could die during those moments,

I would surely find my waterfall.

I could spend eternity with that photograph.

I regained my spirit, found reality once more.

It was such a tender moment.

We both learned. we both grew.

It was real, and we knew.

Dearest Lord, I treasure the gifts you bring me.

I try to learn, to grow, to understand.

These I live for. I pray that you will give me the strength,

the courage, the words to offer those who ask of me.

You are my river, don't ever run dry.

I feel you have given me a glimpse of Heaven.

I have never before felt as I do now.

Help me to be worthy of this precious jewel.

I will polish this radiant spirit each day that

I am able to raise my head from my pillow.

I praise you with all my heart, soul, spirit, and being

for such a tender gift.

Give strength to the butterfly so it may share it's beauty with others.

I slept for a while. I had a dream, it was beautiful.

It was so tender,

I would do it an injustice to try to express it in words.

THANK YOU 7/20/82 11:15 pm

I thought about what we shared tonight, and

I realize how much we grew.

You brought back to me memories of places and times and

people who I had locked away in my private vault for

such a long, long time.

I watched you as you made coffee for me.

I saw you stare into my cup.

You stirred so slowly.

I could feel that you were inside yourself.

I did not want to call you until you were ready to hear again.

The longer I watched you, the more I was touched.

I felt warm.

You brought me so many gifts tonight,

one was a waterfall.

Thank you.

I REMEMBER YESTERDAY 7/23/82 8:14 am

Yesterday, you took me shopping.

I don't think we really went to shop, just to share.

It was so nice not being rushed, taking our time, and

enjoying each other's company.

When I needed rest, you didn't complain,

you just asked where.

We did so many different things yesterday.

I took pictures, I think you did, too.

I like pictures.

I have a picture of two people sitting at a sidewalk cafe.

They are sharing a lunch of potatoes and orange juice, and

they talk of people , and life, and children.

I have a picture of two people sharing thoughts and hopes and dreams.

They are sharing emotions, feelings, with the words of others.

It's not that they don't have their own words,

they just enjoy sharing.

I have a picture of a ray of sun, or maybe it is the warmth of the sun.

This picture exudes emotion.

This picture is very special to me.

It is a gift with a story.

I can never express the feelings or emotions I have shared in that gift.

That gift was a gift of hope, tenderness, joy, and many other

cherished emotions.

That gift resembled a cross.

That cross tells many stories.

I shall try to relate those stories so you may

know the power of that gift.

The cross is the cross which our Christ so desirably bore for us.

That cross is His life among us, His struggles, His battles won.

We should each bear His cross in return.

The raised dot in the center is the Triune,

the completeness of God.

If we are to learn and grow and understand, then

we must hold this Triune as our center.

The ring, or halo about the center is the spirit of the Triune.

We should each allow this spirit to become

the light with which we are able to see,

not just to look.

The rays, leaving the center, illumined by the halo and traveling outward,

are the spirits touched by God, walking, searching, living, and

hoping to find the waterfall.

How I pray that God would allow me to be called as

one of those radiant beams.

This next picture is a mirror,

a reflection of past, present, and tomorrows.

I heard words, or maybe I was dreaming and

wanted to hear those words, which were spoken from the heart.

Lord, I think about how many miles I've walked,

how many clouds I've watched, how many sunny days I've lived, and

I want so deeply, to believe those words.

I've heard the words before, but

they weren't real.

They were spoken by the mouth, not the spirit.

How have I come to be so blessed ?

I want, so much, to be worthy of these gifts.

Lord, as these days I have reserved on this earth pass,

I see your words as they come to life for me.

I now understand how rich I truly am by

storing my jewels in a treasure chest.

You do hold all the keys.

Help me to continue to see your words and to learn,

learn your wants and needs,

to need to fulfill your will.

Help me to help others who ask of me.

I no longer ask myself what I should say to them.

now, I ask you.

I no longer only listen,

I hear and understand.

Lord, You have taught me to not just touch with the hand, but also

to feel with the spirit.

I don't know how to thank you for these gifts.

Lord, I know you will place these photographs into my treasure chest.

I know you will keep them safe.

EARTH, WIND, AND FIRE (the story)

And God created earth so that man might learn.

The earth is the home of man.

It is a vehicle by which mankind may experience and

learn the many lessons which bring mankind closer to God.

There are many roads from which to choose.

Each road leads toward the final rest, the waterfall.

One road teaches of trust, one of love, one of pains.

Upon each lie many bends.

Each bend lives an experience from which to learn and grow.

We are watched and protected by God.

If we become lost for even a moment,

He will answer our cry for help.

If we fall, He is always there to help us up again.

Yes, the roads are long and rough.

We stumble time after time.

We get up and try again.

EARTH, WIND, AND FIRE (the song)

Earth, wind, and fire flame of desire

Lord, lead me to your side

I walk down my road never do tire

I will keep searching led by your light

I know you I've seen you before

Now I will follow you evermore

The earth is your gift from which I might learn

Help me to see life don't let me be blind to your word

I am the wind sent forth by you

I will be your voice till my days are through

You are the fire deep in my soul

Help me to share your warmth with those who are cold

Earth, wind, and fire flame of desire

Lord, lead me to your side

HOLE IN THE SKY 8/9/84 10:40 pm

I had a dream. It seemed real, and may well be.

There was a commotion, a chaos, a feeling of loss.

This was a grand event for those who knew,

for those who understood, for those who had waited.

It took great faith to await this moment,

not knowing when it would come, but

always being ready.

It is difficult to know where to begin, for

this dream had no beginning, it simply always was.

I looked into the sky.

Deep within myself I knew what I was witnessing.

I was awed by the magnificence of what was taking place.

First, the sky was clear, blue as a child's eyes. Then,

without warning, billowing clouds closed in

from all directions, seething and churning.

Finally, there was only one hole in the sky,

encircling the sun.

Then, no sun.

There was a mighty roar,

such as that of innumerable trumpets.

I then looked upon the land.

Some eyes were blind, some eyes were turned upward in awe,

Some eyes were turned upward in elation,

Some eyes were turned away in fear.

I watched, as if in a separate reality,

The mounting excitement, the frenzy, the joy.

It was then that I saw the gloried escort,

as if I had looked into a thousand suns.

The guardians looked across the expanse as if preparing for

a mightier entrance.

Then, as if the universe had exploded,

I saw the arrival of one who was even greater.

Tremendous peace had settled upon me.

I was taken into the midst of the

greatest event of all time.

The event which had been awaited,

had been watched for,

had been prayed for,

my Lord had called us home.

HAVE YOU CARED ENOUGH (a song)

When Jesus knocks upon your door will you answer

When He reaches out to you will you care

When He tells you that He loves you will you listen

Do you even know that He is there

Just call upon my Jesus and you'll know that He is there

When you're down and troubled and you feel nobody cares

Can you stand and tell me that you've seen Him turn away or

Have you never cared enough to look His way

When Jesus says," Come with Me lay down your burdened life."

Will you travel with Him and leave your grief behind

When He says," I'll keep you and I will take your stand."

Will you have the courage to take Him by the hand

Just call upon my Jesus and you'll know that He is there

When you're down and troubled and you feel nobody cares

Can you stand and tell me that you've seen Him turn away or

Have you never cared enough to look His way

FROM HIS HEART TO MY HANDS 12/17/84 5:00 pm (a song)

From His heart to my hands He has blessed me with word and with song

For this I have prayed for and waited it seems for so long

I'd realized that I'd been off the path all along

Instead of listening to the spirit I'd been trying on my own

You've got to learn to let go you've got to

Let the spirit flow like a spring

By yourself you will fall but

You will learn that the Lord can do all things

Lord You've led me down long and hard roads but

Always walked next to me

Lord you've seen me fall time after time but

Always helped me get back on my feet

when I was tired and needed rest you always waited for me

Now ready I'll be waiting for Thee to

Lead me down roads that you choose

Leaning on you listening to you I know I never will lose

I've got to learn to let go

I've got to let the spirit flow like a spring

By myself I will fall but You Lord can do all things

WALK A MILE WITH ME 12/20/84 12:50 pm

I have walked down many roads in sunshine and in rain.

I have seen the agony and I have seen the pain.

I have fallen many times and I have turned away.

now, what I wish to share with you is the never-ending day.

While I traveled in the dark I could not read the signs.

From the shadowed roadside I heard the tortured cries.

Then at a lonely crossroad I heard a pleading voice,

It said," Come this way, out of the dark, evermore rejoice.

Give to me your burden, and I'll give to you this key.

I'll lead you to the lighted path if you will walk a mile with me."

I searched for his footsteps in the rocks and in the sand.

When I found the road too steep He took me by the hand.

He said," Stay close by me and we will soon be there.

This path will not bring to you more than you can bear."

As we journeyed onward the sun began to rise,

I began to see the road we walked and I could see the signs.

I saw the blue sky up above and then I saw His eyes,

full of love which in the dark I could not recognize.

He said," Now travel onward and with this path abide.

You may not see me always, but I'll be ever at your side.

Fear not the crossroads you approach.

Do not hesitate. Remember the path that you must walk is

narrow and is straight."

Again I looked into His eyes, windows they became.

I saw my future in the light, my past was cast away.

Upon His heart I saw the words which He had spoke to me.

I'll remember evermore the message He gave me.

"Give to me your burden and I'll give to you this key.

I'll lead you to the lighted path if you will walk a mile with me."

SOMETIMES (a song) 12/30/84 3:45 pm

Sometimes I don't understand

Why some things get so out of hand

I climb my mountain each day

Don't let clouds stand in my way

Sometimes things aren't so clear

Like why you are still here

With all of my faults

Why do you still call

Still the clouds come

Block out the sun

Lord help me hang on

Till I'm safely home

With You I'll walk

With You I'll talk

With You I'll stand

Precious Lord takes my hand

COUNTRY LANE (a song) 1/30/88

In memory to Gary Vann 'Blue' Thurmond

Country Lane through the trees sunshine through the leaves

I cry when I think of you

Days rush before my eyes as the eagle sails across the sky

I cry when I think of you

Flowers smile as I walk past to be one with the earth is all I ask

I cry when I think of you

Soft breeze on velvet warmth peace within evermore

I cry when I think of you

Take my hand lead me home stay with me don't leave me alone

I cry when I think of you

Endless road time goes on birds sing to the dawn

I cry when I think of you

Again I come to shady glen to be alone with you my friend

I cry when I think of you

JUST BECAUSE YOU ARE

Just because you are kind

Not a facade but from the heart

Just because you are real

Not someone else but yourself

Just because you make me question myself

Not about doubts but of hopes

Just because you remind me of

Walks in the fields

Picking wildflowers

Watching clouds

I COULD SAY

I could say that I like taking long walks

in the country by myself.

That I like sitting at an empty table

watching people walk by.

That I like to sit alone by the water

listening to the sounds of the woods.

That I like to sit by myself

thinking about how my life could have been.

That I like to remember all the times

when I've been alone with myself.

I could say that I like these things, but

I would be lying to myself.

WEAR HIS CROWN

You know that time is running short and

Soon will come that day

When our Savior will return to

Take us all away

Step into the guiding light

Live the way you know is right

Tell the Lord you want to wear His crown

DO I BELIEVE IN DREAMS

You ask me if I believe in dreams.

If you could see inside my heart

you would see only dreams,

dreams of what I wish

my life was.

I have dreams of having happy memories

because I have no happy memories.

I have dreams of sharing my life

with someone who would want to

share their life with me, but

they are only dreams.

I have dreams of walking down a shady lane

sunshine sparkling through the leaves,

hand in hand with a gentle heart, but

no one is there.

I have dreams of being with that special friend,

listening to the trickling stream,

it's music as soft as a butterfly's wings, but

it is only a dream.

I have dreams of moonlight dancing on new fallen snow,

a warm and crackling fire,

sparkling wine of the deepest red,

the woman for whom I would sacrifice my very life,

held securely in my arms, but

again, it is only a dream.

I have dreams of being with that special friend,

standing at the end of the pier,

leaning against the rail,

the sun floating on the edge of the waves,

the sky, crimson and gold, rolling like grains in the field.

Watching sea gulls being gently rocked to sleep

by the ocean's soft lullaby.

Then I remember, it is only a dream.

I see people walking hand in hand,

smiling from deep within their spirit.

I have dreams of being like them, but

they are only dreams.

So long I have waited,

so many times I have prayed for God to

bring someone into my life.

So many times I have wondered if I would ever see that day.

The only way I know to express my deepest feelings

is in my writings.

When I first saw you,

I felt something from deep within your spirit.

I felt drawn to you, not knowing why.

Just being near you,

you have made me feel

good about myself,

good about life,

good about dreams coming true, and

prayers being answered.

I felt that I understood loneliness

better than anyone else could, but

what I felt was merely a hint of what

I feel when I am away from you.

Maybe me being happy,

truly happy,

is yet another dream.

You ask me if I believe in dreams,

it seems that dreams are all I have.

I would find it difficult, but

I would rather be your friend

than to be nothing to you

at all.

DON'T WAIT TOO LATE   (a song)

I sat in the field thinking of you

I watched the sky radiant blue

I saw the flowers colors and hues

I heard the birds singing their tunes

The stream softly flowed by my side

As I listened my heart cried

To share my love I have tried

I felt as though a part of me died

Shadows grow long before my eyes

I've known the pain and I've heard the cries

I've been as free as butterflies

I've been to lands of faraway eyes

My days will soon become dark

Tell me that we shall never part

Each day with you is a new start

You'll always have a place in my heart

Don't wait too late to let me love you

Please know my heart is simple and true

Love is a gift for me and for you

Love is forever I love you

Don't cry for me after I'm gone

My love for you lives ever on

One day again you'll be with me

To walk hand in hand through eternity

So don't wait too late to let me love you

Please know my heart is simple and true

Love is a gift for me and for you

Love is forever I love you

GOLDEN TREE

When I die don't bury me

Just let my spirit fly

Cast my ashes to the wind and

To the open sky

Come take a walk down Country Lane

Look for the golden tree

Sit down relax and close your eyes

Tell me what you see

HEARTACHE (a song)

Loneliness is a heartache no man should feel

His life becomes a fantasy where nothing is real

Memories of days gone by fill his heart

He feels so alone walking in dark

No flowers along the path no birds in the air

He falls to his knees and cries out in despair

Lord I had forgotten you I'd walked away

Now I search within myself for the words to say

Lord please forgive me for all I had done

Lord please tell me I'm still your son

Then I cried tears of joy tears of love

A gentle voice spoke to me from up above

He said see I have not forgotten you

For I have carved you in the palms of my hands

Even though you may wander throughout the land understand

You are mine for eternity though you may fall

I will wait here patiently for you to call out my name

PAINTED LEAVES

Lazy summer afternoon

Lie beneath the trees

Stare into the clear blue sky

Reminisce your dreams

Your eyes are like the rays of sun

Splashed down between the leaves

Your face takes on a peaceful glow

As your spirit leaves

Sail across the golden clouds

Above the tree tops tall

Your eyes become the rainbow of

The painted leaves of fall

I WILL LIVE AGAIN

I've sat in gardens and

Watched the trees dance gently in the wind

I've watched the clouds sail

Silently across the sky

I've listened to the birds

Sing happily to me and

I've thought about emotions that I've known

Peace seemed to come at times

Joy danced around my soul

Sadness came and went again but

Love would make me whole

A hunger in my heart I felt

A gnawing type of pain

I had a need to love someone so

I could live again

Don't wait too late to let me love you

Don't push me away again

The pain I feel will fill my heart and

I will die again

FOR NICOLE

Turning back the pages of life's everyday

Wondering what yesterday was meant for

Reflecting on the memories of feelings long departed

I'm wondering what tomorrow will bring

I've met people who were some place lost

In a void and time unknown

I've met people whom I've seemed to know before

I've met people who were complacent in their lives

I've met people who have opened up their doors

I think about the places and the times that I

Have known and I reason out why I am here and now

I wonder why people care and

Why they come and go and

Feel things will soon work out somehow

As for friends that I cannot seem to live without their trust

I easily can make this statement clear

For it is friends like you that keep me warm and

Hoping for the best and for you

I cry a silent happy tear

YOU NEED NOT SAY WHY

The sun will set and the moon will rise

The artist paints the autumn skies

Days will come and days will go

The rivers never cease to flow

Fresh are the flowers and green is the grass

But these things will soon come to pass

Try once more and you will see

The sun will shine and the birds will sing

ODE TO ONE I NEVER KNEW

We traveled down a sunny road

Though we did never meet

Birds sang flowers shone

The waters cooled our feet

Life then was good to us

We had never cried

Days were warm nights were cool

We chased butterflies

We had hopes so beautiful

They were beyond compare

How could we have ever known

Our sorrow we would share

We had met upon a dusty road

As the storm brewed overhead

We had no idea where to go

Our hearts were filled with dread

We walked on hand in hand

Till the sun had lit up the sky

Birds began to sing again

Our hearts had ceased to cry

ONE MORE TIME AGAIN

I'd like to see the sunrise

On the sparkling dewy dawn

I'd like to see the beauty of a

newborn spotted fawn

I'd like to see the laughter in

The happy children's eyes

I'd like to see the stretching wings

as the eagle flies

I'd like to see the rainbow from

A gentle summer's rain

I'd like to see all these things

Just one more time again

PARADISE

I found myself seeking many things this world could not provide

I felt as though a blind man feels my pain was locked inside

Questions I had too many of the answers I could not find

Jesus touched my heart that day and told me to look inside

The love that I was seeking must rise from within my soul

to blossom as a flower toward all that I behold

I had a dream of Paradise it touched me to my soul

The flowers seemed as colored lights the streets were paved with gold

The path I walked led round about the gardens and the trees and

at the end the man I saw was my Lord waiting for me

REMEMBERING THE FORGOTTEN

So many feelings and emotions,

so long ago locked away

forgotten even their existence.

Some place in another time and

space they were so full of life.

then gone to be known no more.

You brought me something which

you may not have even known,

a spark of who I used to be.

Such a gentle voice, I've needed to hear,

of patience,

of tenderness,

of kindness to my spirit.

You caused the bonds of my darkness

to relax it's cold grasp,

allowing flashes into my past.

You made me feel emotions

long forgotten,

long denied,

long ago locked away.

You caused me to feel needed,

wanted,

cared for,

as if I had worth.

So many things I had forgotten,

put aside in fear of

being hurt again.

I made myself believe that

if I did not feel,

I would not be hurt.

I believe myself to be strong in spirit,

striving for truths,

always seeking to learn.

I hid my fears behind a mask,

denying my emotions even to

my aching heart.

I made myself believe if I kept

myself closed from those around me,

they could not touch me.

They would not see inside my heart,

laugh at my fears,

hurt me again.

Pain that I've known has caused me

to pray for death,

to pray for escape.

I fear rejection so I do not allow myself

to be in a place where

I can be its target.

I fear not finding peace within my heart,

so I made myself to feel nothing.

If I no longer allow my emotions to arise,

I no longer have to guard them.

Somehow, you have broken down a wall

I've built so long ago.

You have reached inside me.

I don't know how to handle the

emotions you have caused me to remember.

I don't even know if I should

allow myself to remember.

What would it gain.

What do I do with these broken pieces,

fragments of someone I used to be.

Should I allow myself the happiness

I've so long ago denied,

even if only within myself.

Should I put those parts of me away,

for now, forever,

and be content with

not remembering the forgotten.

SILENCE CAN BE SO HEAVY

Sometimes I sit, and wait,

not even knowing why.

Sometimes I wonder if I should.

Sometimes my mind drifts

on clouds of memories, but

it seems most are memories of emptiness,

of being alone,

of being some place,

somewhere in time.

I try to remember what came

before the darkness, but

nothing.

It is as though the emptiness has always been

the whole of my life.

At times I almost see pictures of my past,

not quite focused, and

watch them fade away into the

twilight from which they came.

They are like shadows in the waves.

At times I cry out into the winds,

no one to hear,

no one to know,

no one to care.

At times I wonder why.

At times I don't want to know.

At times I ask myself where am I,

where am I going.

The pain can be as the thunder deafening my ears,

as lightning blinding my eyes.

At times, silence can be so heavy.

SHOWERS OF LIGHT

Letting go of lives past I found myself drifting on

Warm rays from the sun

Feeling my daydreams

Become one with my soul.

Beams of light rained down

Like robes of glowing white.

Showers of light like rain.

In the clouds I saw In the midst of such peril,

An oasis of love in the

Face of our Lord.

Young was His look, with eyes of crystalline blue.

He touched me with His heart.

I felt the love within.

MOUNTAIN STREAM

Dedicated to Ron Ensley

Mountain stream

Crystal clear water flowing forever

Cool and sweet flowing forever

Song of the birds ringing of the bells

Ring in my spirit

Sing of the tales my sylvan dream

Send me your word I long to hear

You like the stream from the earth flows

Lasting forever

Feed my spirit with your love

Clouds fly overhead

There is no death only life

Blue sky mirror the ocean

Stretching far as the eye can see

Sunset pastel gold

Stories untold

Send me your crimson

Show me the power

Paint my sky

Smell the flower

Feel the bumblebee

Walk with me barefoot on soft grass

Wipe my gentle tear

I know you are here

Stream cool and sweet to my lips

Your voice is soft as the breeze

Touch the leaves

Soft fur of the fawn

Show me your dawn

show me your dawn

With the sunrise look into my eyes

Smile on me

Walk hand in hand on your path

Lead me to the water

Lead me to the spring

Let me drink of your spirit

Let me fly on your clouds

Let me be with you evermore

Evermore

SOMEWHERE IN THE DARK

Loneliness is waking up in the morning and

not remembering how long

you've been waking up alone.

Loneliness is driving down the road and

turning to talk to someone then

remembering there is no one there.

Loneliness is sitting at a corner table

not really feeling like eating and

just staring out the window.

Loneliness is wanting someone to

be there with you and for you and

realizing there is no one there.

Loneliness is walking along the stream

feeling emotions and knowing there is

no one there to share them with you.

Loneliness is wanting someone to talk to and

wondering if there was

do you still remember how.

Loneliness is watching the rain and

hearing every drop

as it taps against your window.

Loneliness is forgetting how many times

you've gone to work then home because

there was nothing else in your life.

Loneliness is realizing that

you smile on the outside because

you've forgotten how to smile inside.

Loneliness is wondering why you

get up each morning when

you have nothing to look forward to.

Loneliness is realizing that you

don't remember the last time you made plans

because there was no one to make plans with.

Loneliness is caring too much for someone with whom

you know you cannot be.

Loneliness is seeing that person

with the smiling eyes and

wishing they were smiling for you.

Loneliness is crying tears inside your heart

knowing that no one sees them

except yourself.

Loneliness is being somewhere in the dark and

realizing that you are in the same place in the light.

TEARS OF SORROW TEARS OF JOY

Sitting watching the rain

Like tears of sorrow from the sky

I wonder how many times that

I have caused my dear Savior to cry

Staring through steamy windows

Looking past busy streets

I remember days gone by

Days filled with defeats

I see times when I should have cried out to Him

Knowing He would care but always feeling bare

In a world full of sin

Adrift on a never ending sea

I found no star to guide me

No dove to lead me to dry land

No sun to show me east from west

Days without end nights without sleep

I came to know I was lost

Not because I knew not the way but

Because I did not seek

I stretched my hands to the skies

Tears in my eyes and I prayed

Lord take me away from the deep

Teach me to keep you in my heart

Help me to change your tears of sorrow

To tears of joy

VISIONS THROUGH THE WINE

Silently thinking alone in my world

Sounds sinking slowly into pools of smoke

Journeys through the mind

Journeys through the past as

I stare into the crystal of the

Sparkling glass of wine

WHERE DO YOU GO

When a teardrop hits the bottom of your heart

So loud it drowns out the thunder

Of the world,

Where do you go ?

When you can see birds singing and

Can't hear their song,

Where do you go ?

When you can see the flowers and

Can't feel their joy,

Where do you go ?

When you can see where the wind has been and

Can't feel its coolness,

Where do you go ?

When you can see the footprints down the land and

No one is there anymore,

Where do you go ?

When you can sing the songs and

Can't hear the music anymore,

Where do you go ?

When you look up into blue sky full of sunshine and

Can't feel its warmth,

Where do you go ?

When you sit alone and

Can't feel the pain anymore,

Where do you go ?

When you reach out and No one is there anymore,

Where do you go ?

When you open your eyes and

All you see is emptiness,

Where do you go ?

When you cry and

There are no more tears,

Where do you go ?

I stare into my coffee

Watching the steam rise and disappear

Like so many dreams and hopes that I've had.

I think about happy times when I could smile and

I could laugh and

Now are only memories.

I think about sad times when I could hurt and I could feel and

I could cry.

I watch as life seems so far away

Like the sun in the horizon

Slowly sinking out of sight and

I wonder.

Why do I sit and wait ?

What am I waiting for ?

Life will not return, but still,

I wait, not knowing, not wanting,

Not feeling.

Will I ever feel again ?

Do I want to feel again ?

Do I want to care again ?

The world seems to be leaving me.

I have tried to give and

I have given all I am.

Now, when I need,

No one can hear my cries so

Why do I cry still ?

If only once more peace would hold me

In it's arms as it is now comforting the night

But, peace will not come and

It really does not matter anymore.

WE FELT PEACE

We were walking hand in hand through the sand and

We were talking.

Every now and then we'd turn around

To see where we had been, and

Then we'd look to see where we were going.

We spoke of many times when we would laugh or

Find ourselves crying,

Trying to put broken pieces back together,

Finding fortune in misfortune,

Finding answers to the questions,

Growing wiser.

We stood on the bank as the sun set on the water,

Golden waves came to greet us

As we pondered on the power of the moment.

It seemed that time stood still.

An eternity had come and gone,

We couldn't stay.

So we walked across the field

Watching birds play with the flowers and

We felt peace.

WHY (a song)

Why Lord do I feel so alone

Why Lord does home not feel like home

I search your path every day

In hopes that you will smile my way

Touch my heart that I may always believe

I seek your word I seek your truth

You know I walk in faith needing no proof

When I don't see your light

How do I know what is right

Touch my eyes that I may always see

Why Lord am I sometimes confused

Sometimes feeling broken wrongly accused

The nearer I get to you

The farther I seem to be

Touch my feet that I may always follow you

Why Lord am I sometimes afraid

To walk the path you walked solely on faith

Lord You know my choice is to

Always hear your voice

Touch my ears that I may hear your call

CHORUS :

Lord teach me to walk in your light

Teach me to know right from wrong

Lord we welcome your coming again

We pray it won't be too long

WINDOW TO THE PAST

I sat at a table and watched

through a window.

Everyone and everything I saw

made me feel I was

looking through a window to the past.

I remembered how lonely

my life really was.

How I longed for someone to be with me,

sometimes to talk,

sometimes to listen,

sometimes just to be there.

I pretended in my mind

how happy I would be.

THE SIMPLEST WORDS

Dedicated to Cindy

Sometimes it is the simplest words

Which tell a more complete story.

You don't always need a lot of pretty words,

Flowery talk,

Dramatics or imagery.

You don't always need brilliant blue skies or

Fluffy white clouds.

You don't always need flowers

Gracefully dancing in the midday sun, or

Raindrops tapping against

Your window on a cold and

Lonely night.

You don't always need to hear

Children's laughter

Like music on the wind.

Sometimes, just a smile

Can say so much more.

A COMFORTING HAND

Many times I think of you and all the gifts you bring

You've brought me smiles and happy times

New songs for me to sing

I can see you sitting there by the

Gently flowing stream

Flowers adorn your glowing smile

You are the picture of Spring

The birds sing their songs only for you

They dance in the air a ballet

The gentle breeze blows through your hair

The butterflies love to play

I've wanted so much to give to you

To help you see through new eyes

All of the beauty there is to behold

All the warm tender feelings of life

It seems with all that you've given to me

The gifts that I have to share

Are not of the splendor of which you are due and

Cannot even compare

If I've made you happy or I've made you smile

I thank you for receiving that gift

If I've done nothing for you at all

Please find it in your heart to forgive

It's been too long since someone had let

Me try to bring happiness to their heart

When I try so hard and always seem to fail

It tears my soul apart

Just smile for me and say it's okay

Deep inside I understand

I'm always in the wrong place and time

Reaching for a comforting hand

THE GARDEN GREEN (a song)

When I've reached my journey's end and

I say goodbye to you my friend

I'll take my walk across the sky

to a land where dreams shall never die

In my travels through this life

I've found that dreams are make believe

In the land I go to now

Dreams become reality

It's like a magic wonderland

It's so hard to explain but

You will understand all things

When you travel on that plane

The colors seem illumined by

Some strange and inner light

Radiance beyond compare

Like a million stars at night

Smile for me and wish me well

As I go on to greater quests

Finally the peace I seek

Is what this passage brings to me

I hope I've helped you find some things

You had buried in your past

The time I was given to be with you

I knew would too soon come to pass

We are all travelers on this plane

One day we will reunite

In the splendor of Garden Green

In the soft and warm sunlight

CHORUS :

When we meet again in Garden Green

By the waterfall of endless dreams

We'll carry on our journey once more

Walking along the distant shore

HOW CAN I MAKE YOU KNOW (a song)

For so long now I've waited in the shadows

Desiring the love you give another man

So many times I've wanted to be there

Standing beside you holding your hand

So many times I've waited and wondered

If I'd get the chance to offer to you

The love and affection of which you are worthy

The respect and the honor which are long overdue

We both have walked through our mountains and valleys

Bathed in the sunshine and stood in the rain

I'd like to bring you the happiness you search for

We both have had our share of the pain

I don't know how you feel about me

The thoughts that I have or the way that I feel

I hope you know the things that I tell you

Are not just words but beliefs that are real

CHORUS :

What I am asking is for the chance to be

Loving and kind and concerned for your needs

To walk in your sunshine in the light of your day

To be there beside you when your skies turn to gray

REMINISCING ON COUNTRY LANE

Melancholy days are such a treasured gift

Allowing us to sit back and reminisce of

Times gone by, old friends we haven't seen in years.

I like to remember walks I've taken down Country Lane.

I can still see the long and narrow lane,

The hard packed sand under my feet, and

The loosely strewn pebbles.

The trees on each side stretch overhead

Making a canopy from the sun, but

Still allowing small sunbeams to

Filter down through the leaves.

I remember the golden tree.

I used to sit beneath its protective boughs

Writing my emotions and playing my music

To all who would listen.

I remember the many thoughts I had while walking,

Thoughts of loneliness at times,

Thoughts of peace at others,

Thoughts of missing someone I had not yet met.

Country Lane was a friend to me.

No matter how I was feeling,

Happy or sad,

Country Lane was always patient and kind,

Always had time to listen.

SUNRISE OF THE NEW DAWN (a song)

If I only had one wish I'd wish for you

My only life I'd give for you

The starlight in your eyes lights up my dark

The power of your love fills my heart

If I only had one dream I'd dream of you

You turn my skies from gray to blue

If I only had one song I'd sing of you

All of my thoughts are pictures of you

If I only had one tear I'd cry for you

A tear of joy was never so true

If I only had one smile I'd smile for you

The peace I feel deep in my soul comes from you

CHORUS :

Life cannot give to me

The happiness which you bring

You are the sunrise of the new dawn

WHERE DID YOU FIND THE KEY (a song)

I took a walk today out in the field

I thought about the happiness you cause me to feel

I saw the smile on your face the stars in your eyes

I felt your love for me and started to cry

My heart has never before felt joy such as this

The petal of the rose was never as soft as your kiss

I can't think of anything other than you

I didn't know that I could love as much as I love you

I think about the things you say and wonder inside

Am I really seeing what's real am I really alive

How did you find those things that I'd locked away

The answers to these questions I cannot say

You have opened my eyes to a world I never knew

I've never before felt the love I feel from you

Tell me I'm not creating a dream from thin air

Tell me that for me you really do care

I burn a candle for you in my room every night

It reminds me of your eyes and their sparkling starlight

I feel the warmth which comes from deep in your soul

The love you give to me makes me feel whole

CHORUS :

Tell me where did you find the key

To unlock the door to my inner self

Tell me how did you find those things

I had hidden up high on the shelf

May be you always had the magic

deep within your soul

The missing part of my waterfall

The peace that would make me whole

EVEN WHEN IT RAINS

Even when the skies bring rain

Know that God smiles upon you

For with a happy heart

Every day is beautiful

WHAT YOU DIDN'T SAY

So many times we must read between the lines

Not just to see what is clear to the eye but also

What is kept within

When the rains come we must look

Between the raindrops to see the sunshine

When we walk through the forest we must

Look between the trees to see the leaves

When we hear a bird sing we must

look between it's songs to see the

happiness in its heart

As we go through life we must

Look between the hard times to

See what we have learned

I have read between the lines and

Understand what you said but

didn't say

I've heard you say

what you didn't say

countless times in my heart

BATTLE SCARRED BOAT (A SONG)

I've found that life can be so unkind

When the world knows you're in troubled times

So many times I've been beaten down

I feel like an ocean with no sound

The turmoil I keep locked deep within

Causes my spirit to grow very dim

I try not to let anyone see

Just how vulnerable I can be

How many times can I stay afloat

With a barely seaworthy battle scarred boat

It seems that the evening of my life draws near

With no sight of land or safety of pier

Again I shall close my eyes to sleep

And wonder if my life shall enter the deep

As long as there will be hope of dry land

I shall look always for your reaching hand

CHORUS :

Though my sails now are billowed and fast

I still have the fear that this blessing will pass

In the past I have struggled and fared out the storm

Slept from the battle with my spirit worn

LAY ME TO REST

Lay me to rest in a watery grave

My mind is imprisoned my soul is enslaved

My life has been shattered my troubles they're many

As for the answers I haven't got any

When I speak there is no sound

When I need you you're not around

You seem not to love me but maybe you do

Why can't you show me or give me a clue

Won't you lay me to rest in a watery grave

So the sea winds can carry my spirit away

LOST

Sometimes I get so lost in my thoughts that words won't come

music won't come

peace won't come.

I walk not seeing the path I follow,

the blue of the sky, or

the flowers in the grass.

I can see birds in the trees, but

no longer hear their songs,

feel the joy in their hearts, or

the happiness in their eyes.

Sometimes I get so lost in my thoughts that

I cannot find myself.

I FEEL SO ALONE

I never knew days could be so empty or hours so long or

quiet so heavy.

In the past when I felt lost I always knew there was

some place I could go.

It doesn't seem that way any longer.

In the past when I was lonely I could find a crowd to be in and

still be alone in a crowd.

I feel like a night without stars,

a bird without song,

a field without flowers.

I feel so alone.

THE EMPTINESS INSIDE

Each writing is like a new leaf on my tree,

so many different colors I see.

Some of anger,

some of bliss,

some of painful loneliness.

Some of joy and some of love

some about our Lord above.

Right now the emotions that I feel are

sharp as knives and painfully real.

I feel as though I am empty inside,

lost in a lost world with no place to hide.

How can I make you understand the truth of the

emptiness I feel when

I'm away from you.

TEACH ME (a song)

Lord Lord teach me to pray

Help me keep the dark away

Shine your light on me today

Don't let me go astray

Lord Lord teach me to see

Christ like harmony

Show me that in us you live

Show me that our past you forgive

Lord Lord teach me to hear

All the many silent tears

Shed by angels of the cross

For those of us still lost

Lord Lord teach me to speak

Let my voice not be weak

Let me praise you with my song

Keep my faith in you as strong

Lord Lord teach me to sing

Let me praise you in everything

Let me sing my songs to you

If others listen You'll hear too

Lord Lord teach me to be

More like you less like me

Wash me with your cleansing blood

Baptize me with your love

Lord Lord teach me to see

Christ like harmony

Show me that our past you forgive

Show me that in us you live

DEATH

As I lie here, awaiting the steely, cold hands of death,

I grow old and weak.

With every passing moment death walks slowly toward me with

revenge in his voice as he

talks of things to come.

He is coming ever closer and his footsteps are

getting heavy as he is

wondering which door to lead me through.

He has arrived.

As I close my eyes I wonder if he will surprise me.

He takes me by the hand and I go,

wondering if I will grow stronger with the passing.

He leads me down a dark passageway full of doors

so dark and gray.

I wonder when he will stop.

We continue, seemingly for days.

As my eyes constantly gaze at the never changing walls.

We stop and face a door, so pale and gray,

scented with decay.

We stand there for endless moments as

he opens the door with a nod,

for he is God.

THE PRISONER

Last night I sat and watched the wind.

I leaned against the tree and I thought about happy times, and

sad times,

times with my friends, and

times I spend alone.

I relived many emotions.

I relived many dreams which never seem to come true.

I came to realize that I am a prisoner.

I always believed myself to be a free person,

free to come and go,

no one to answer to, but

I was wrong.

I was a prisoner of my loneliness.

I remembered all the times I wanted someone to come home to,

someone to talk to,

someone to listen to, but

no one was ever there.

I watched the wind blow, and I wondered,

does the wind feel the same as I.

Is the wind as empty as I ?

When I met you, I looked into your eyes, and I wondered,

how can you seem to be so happy ?

I could see in your eyes such deep emotion,

such tender feelings.

There was something in your eyes that said you are true and real,

someone not afraid of your true emotions.

I looked at myself and I realized I was wearing a

mask of happiness.

I felt that I was lying to myself.

I never felt true happiness until I met you.

You make me feel that you can look inside me,

that you could see the hurt and pain which

tears at my spirit.

I felt you cared, but

I knew not why.

I was afraid, afraid of rejection.

I loved someone, once, a long time ago.

She said she would always be at my side.

One day, facing a great wall,

I found myself alone.

The pain was so deep, I could not allow myself to

become close to anyone again.

Even death would have been welcome.

I felt I was living my hell in life itself.

When I met you I became afraid.

I cared for you, not knowing why.

You made me happy inside.

You made me feel wanted.

Last night I watched the wind blow, and I thought of you.

THE LEAST OF THESE (a song)

The hungry line up daily blindly get their meal.

It seems they go through motions no longer able to feel.

The homeless lie in doorways forgotten by their kind.

The thirsty find their solace in a bottle of cheap wine.

Can your heart be saddened can your tears for them flow?

Do you feel a need to help them,

do you even want to know?

In Christ we all are brothers,

we creatures great and small.

It's not how tall a man stands,

it's how a man stands tall.

Reach out your hand in charity,

reach out your hand in hope.

Reach out with your heart and soul,

help them learn to cope.

As we do for these the least

we do also for our Lord.

How can you sit there watching as

the world dies in discord?

Walk down the alley and open up your eyes.

Listen my brother to the lonesome, painful cries

of a world in pain and sorrow

of a world in agony.

Cry for them, my brother, for they no longer see.

THE VALLEY OF SHADOWS

I walked in the Valley of Shadows for so long.

I walked in darkness, I walked alone.

A voice cried out to me in my despair.

He said my son I love you.

He said my child I care.

TEARS IN THE MIRAGE

Mountains roll like waves on the sea.

Patches of fields, the smell of the trees.

Sunsets over valleys and glens,

rises again on dew glistening.

Clouds sail on like ships in the wind.

Birds sing their songs so I may listen again.

The smell of the clover fills the air.

A little more solitude,

I'm almost there.

Each bend in the road brings sadness to me.

I strain to look, but cannot see.

Each mirage is a memory.

I had never known pain within me so

until I had known the pain of being alone

without you.

THE POWERS OF GIFTS

I wish you could know the happiness you bring by the gifts you give,

by allowing me to make you happy,

by the smile on your face.

I learned a lesson of gifts long ago,

a lesson of the powers of giving and receiving.

One gift cannot be compared to another.

There is first the power of giving,

the thoughts,

the emotions,

the joy and the love felt by the one who gives.

There is also the joy that person feels by

making someone happy.

There is also the power in the receiving of the gift,

the happiness, the joy,

the feeling of being cared about

the feeling of being loved.

The value of one gift cannot be compared to another.

The value is in the joy in the giving

in the receiving.

I cannot know how great is your joy, and

you cannot know how great is mine.

You cannot know how much happiness you have brought to me.

You cannot know how much you make me feel wanted,

needed,

cared about,

loved.

You cannot know how much I miss you,

how empty I am without you,

how much I need to see you smile.

SONG ON THE BREEZE

My life is full of loneliness for all that I behold

There is no warmth my heart's grown cold.

Stand in the doorway smile at me.

My heart is chained by memories.

Song on the breeze teach me to cope.

Teach me of life teach me of hope.

Take this dark mask from my eyes.

Teach me to live not to die.

Teach my heart to love again.

Walk by me look my way.

Turn my night into day.

Don't let me be alone.

Fill my heart with your song.

Song on the breeze sing me a tune

Tell me of sunshine and tell me of rainbows and

skies that are blue.

Song on the breeze tell me of truth.

Tell me of feeling and emotional being and

hopes that are new.

I CRY FOR MANDY (a song)

I have tried to say I love you in so many different ways

My heart longs for you my nights run into days

into days

Where do I go when my roads all seem to end

You are the one I call my friend

my friend

Don't walk out don't turn away

I know that I have made mistakes that was yesterday

yesterday

Without you I'm not complete and there is not a dark storm

I can defeat without you

Please look inside your heart and find the love to forgive

Please don't take my life let me give it to you

so we may start anew fresh as the rain with

sunshine and rainbows

no more pain

no more pain

Now I cry a silent tear into the wind

I pray that you will find the grace to accept my love again

again

I cry for Mandy I cry for love

I pray the spirit will descend as a snow white dove and

teach me to fly above the clouds

teach me to walk in faith

no more doubts

no more doubts

ONE STANDS ALONE

Amidst the beauty of creation

Atop a mountain crest

Independent of tradition

Outcast by the rest

Demanding of attention

Deserving of respect

He stands alone in honor

Of what he represents

I WONDER WHY

As I go through life, I sometimes wonder why.

Why do I go on, what am I searching for.

Have I found it or do I believe, deep inside, that

I never will.

I paid my dues, but why am I still paying, and for what.

I feel like I'm walking in circles going nowhere.

Time really has no meaning for me anymore.

I come, I go, I seek, but

I never seem to find.

When I feel like I've found happiness, it is like

a picture on the wall.

I can look at it, but I still cannot live in its reality.

It is like dreams.

Dreams are all I have, but

where is the reality.

What is my reality.

Where do I go from here.

Why should I go on.

PRAISE ON

A tale as told by the birds from the Waterfall

Sing, cry the birds of the wood.

Sing happily to the sunrise of a new day,

a dawning of a free spirit,

a redeeming of a life.

Sing until the hearts of love rejoice.

Raise your voice in song.

Praise each and every living creature.

Praise the skies above.

Sing glory till forever is no more,

to the God who gave you love.

Praise on.

For every living creature has a soul that cannot die.

It is made of happy smiles and it is made of painful cries.

Praise the Father in Heaven, for

He knows the place and time when

we shall leave this world of ours and

forever be with Him.

Praise on.

STEPPING STONES   (a spoken song)

The frets upon my guitar are the stepping-stones I've laid.

They remind me of my trials and the mistakes that I've made,

all the learning that I've done and all the tears I've cried,

all the happiness and fears that I keep locked inside.

The strings are roads that I have traveled down.

I know they lead some place, and I'll continue on my journey

until I find the peace that waits for me and

stays for me at least within my heart

till one day from this journey

I will suddenly depart.

The face of my guitar is light and darker blue

reminding me of happy times that I have had with you,

reminding me that love is endless as the open sky and

that knowing you and loving you that I shall never die.

The keys are keys of life I've found while

walking along the path.

The lessons I've learned are deep within my heart

till eternity shall pass.

So sing the songs of the Waterfall to those who listen long.

Tell the tales of the Waterfall with deep and endless song.

Never fear tomorrow, for tomorrow never comes.

It's just an endless journey until this life is done.

Until this life is done.

I AM AN EMPTY VESSEL

I am an empty vessel.

I was filled with love and sunshine, but

I was broken and have been drained of my thoughts and emotions.

I am an empty vessel.

I walk inside my mind, searching for some lost fragment of reality, but

I am lost in a dark void.

I was like a balloon.

I could not release my thoughts and my seams burst.

I could no longer contain my spirit.

I have sprung free and I am spanning the planes of time and space.

I shall return soon.

THE TRAVELLER

He came, some say, from far away, but did he come from a place, or

a time.

He came with a purpose.

He knew his time was short and

this only served to

strengthen his fight.

He brought a message for one, and

that one did not listen.

Time continued and he realized that the one to hear

could not listen until the traveler travels on.

The day grew closer when the journey would resume.

When the traveler is gone and

only memories remain,

then can the listener hear.

IT BREAKS MY HEART (a song)

It breaks my heart to hear children cry,

tears of sorrow in their eyes.

It breaks my heart when the sun won't shine and

it seems there is no end to time.

It breaks my heart when I cannot see

flowers waving in the breeze.

It breaks my heart when I cannot feel

emotions I once knew were real.

NOTHING LEFT TO BURN

When I look around the world and loneliness I see

I wonder why I go on striving endlessly

Life has been an uphill climb the top I cannot reach

The clouds have closed around me like the ocean on the beach

I've given all I have to give with nothing in return

I've lived off my emotions till there's nothing left to burn

Why am I alone reaching for a dream

I'll never see come true

Why am I alone sitting in the darkness of

wishing I could be with you

You're always speaking of many things neither here nor there

I try to say I love you but you just don't seem to care

My love for you will always live deep within my soul

I've cried until I could not feel the sorrow anymore

I've always waited for your love

it's busy some place else

Your love for me stays in your heart you have

no need of mine I've felt

WALKING DOWN THE ROAD AT NIGHT

I like to walk down the road at night.

I have time for myself.

Time to think.

Time to remember.

Time to relive emotions dear to me.

When I see the many colors of

lights glowing through colored curtains and

the lights of front porches with the moths flying in circles

I remember all the Christmases my father

would drive us around to see the many colored lights of

happiness and joy.

I like to hear dogs barking into the darkness.

The barking follows you as you go.

One of my favorite memories is the smell of wood burning

in the fireplace.

I remember going camping, the smell of the fire,

bacon cooking in a sizzling pan, and

the smell of dew on the morning grass.

HONEYSUCKLE AND FIRESKY (a song)

I had almost forgotten

How sweet is the scent honeysuckle

Soft and sweet it floats upon gentle breeze

It takes me back to

Carefree days and peaceful nights

I looked up to the sky

It was a fire sky

Teardrops in the red wine

Why when life had so much to give

Was I destined to live

All alone with no one to stand by my side

I had almost forgotten

How sweet is the scent honeysuckle

Honeysuckle

Honeysuckle

SHATTERED REFLECTIONS

In memory of Wade

Clear, blue sky cracked by darkened clouds

Lonely people who hide in crowds

Birds that don't fly or sing

Sadness covers everything

One-room apartments with dirty, bare walls

Old run down buildings with dark, narrow halls

Moonlight shines on a dust-covered chair

That nobody cleans because nobody cares

He sits by himself to reminisce

He wonders how he got like this

The sadness crushes his very soul

It causes his mind to feel very old

Now he has no more illusions

Only his life's shattered reflections

He now stands at the window and stares below

At the city covered with dirty snow

He's thinking of loneliness,

The closest friend he's found as

He steps from the window and

Falls to the ground.

I CRY MY OWN TEARS

At times I think and I hurt.

I hurt because I have not found a way to tell you

how much I love you.

I think of all the things you do,

all the ways you say you love me, and

I cry my own tears.

I struggle to say I love you, but

there are no sounds.

I cry my own tears.

THE PATH I WALK

The path I walk is mine alone.

Every turn brings more to me and

at each I rest and learn.

Those stumbling blocks along the way are mine

from which to learn and

be wiser than before.

The pits and meadows teach me and

I learn to be.

When I come to the end I will not fear for

I have learned to love God.

SHOES I CANNOT FILL

I once journeyed with a man.

We visited many places, many peoples,

many times.

We saw rivers of crystal clear water,

trees of green and

flowers of every color.

We listened to birds singing as they thrived in their

happy sunshine filled lives.

We sat under trees and watched fluffy white clouds as

they sailed across the sky.

We imagined many things in their ever-changing shapes and peaks.

We talked with many people from many lands and

many places of the mind and

of the heart.

People who were all so different, but

then again, they were all so much alike.

I once journeyed with a man whose spirit seemed to flow.

As He walked His feet were light as wind upon the snow.

All He owned He carried as a shirt upon His back, but

there was nothing of this world for which He felt a lack.

He taught me much of life as we traveled day by day, and

when we'd come upon a stranger He would teach me what to say.

From Him I learned to listen not merely just to hear.

He taught me how to smile from the heart and

how to shed a tear.

He taught me how to look upon this world in which we live.

From Him I learned not to take, but that I was to give.

Now I journey with a man whose shoes I cannot fill.

I search along the road we walk for ways to do His will.

He helps me move the mountains with gentle, loving care.

He fills my heart with leaves of life to remind me that He cares.

WHO WILL LISTEN

When I sing my songs to the winds where do they go ?

When I play my music to the trees who will listen ?

When I need to talk it seems there is no one to hear my plea.

When I am lonely it seems there is no one to be with me.

There is no pain as great as a lonely heart.

There is no place as empty as a lonely life.

There is no desert as barren as a love which cannot be shared.

I CAN'T FIND THE WORDS

I remember times when I was so empty.

I remember times when I felt so alone.

I remember times when my heart cried strongly.

I remember times when I had no home.

I remember times of walking in circles with nothing more to lose and

nothing to gain.

I remember being alone with only my sorrows and

all of my pains.

I can't find the words to tell you my feelings, but

my memories cannot compare with

the emptiness and loneliness I've come to know when

I need you and you're not there.

REASON ENOUGH

When you told me to smile I said give me a reason.

Forgive my selfish nature, for

you just being

is reason enough.

A SMILE FOR YOU

You are the only one I can smile for.

I GIVE YOU THE SUNSHINE

I give you the sunshine to warm your days,

the mellowness of its golden rays.

I give you the green leaves in the spring of the year,

remembrance of rebirth, a silent tear.

I give you the flowers of all colors and hues, the

cheerful song of the morning lark's tunes.

I give you the skies of crystalline blue,

a summer's rain so gentle and cool.

I give you the memories of the happiness you bring,

the sound of the bell with its faraway ring.

The gifts you have given me I hold dearly within so that

maybe someday I can feel them again.

I WONDER IF SHE KNOWS

As I sit here, contemplating on my life,

past and present,

I wonder of the future.

I think of the life's experiences I have lived through.

I am reminded of crises and outcomes of

less pleasurable circumstances.

The illness, the treatments,

the emotional and psychological side effects

which no one seems to notice, except myself.

At such a young age, I passed through hellish tortures

I could not choose to return to in the present.

Surgery is a frightening event,

not knowing if you will wake up again, or if you do,

if you will be better than before, or worse.

I remember dying during my last surgery.

I wonder why I was revived.

Was it the right thing to do ?

I remember the loss of my friends because

they were not able to accept the seriousness of my health.

I remember people who tried to be my friend

because of my sickness, not because of me as a person.

I remember friends I have made along the way because of

who I was, and who I am.

I can see pictures of memories, both god and bad.

I can see some memories as if I had lived them just yesterday.

I remember the hurt, the loneliness,

the physical pain, the anger.

I can still feel the rejection, for it is rejection that

I fear the most.

All else is meaningless in comparison.

I have learned many lessons throughout my life.

I have learned that the eternal search for truths is

the path I should walk.

I have learned that to not seek truth is to lie to ourselves and

to all those with whom we come in contact.

My enemies of loneliness and fear of rejection

have haunted me for many years now.

I often wonder why so many people are able to

find their life partner,

someone to love and to be loved by,

someone to care for and to be cared for in return.

I also see many people who are taken for granted by their partner.

So many people abused emotionally, spiritually,

psychologically, physically.

Why, when they have so much love to give,

are they imprisoned by their mate ?

Why are they not loved as they should be,

respected as they should be,

nurtured as they should be ?

It pains my heart so very much to see someone

throw their love into the wind.

For I have also loved someone who could not love me in return.

I have also loved someone who did care,

who did make me feel needed, wanted, loved, but,

could not share that love with me.

She has made me happy beyond compare.

She has brought me such wonderful gifts, but

does not accept that she has brought me such happiness.

She has made my heart sing with songs

I never knew I could sing.

There is such power in her gifts, but

she can't see it because she has been denied so strongly

in her own life.

She has been made to feel as if she is not important, or

needed, or wanted, or loved.

I wish that I could be allowed the chance to show her

just how special she is,

how important she is,

how wanted and needed and loved she is.

When all I could see were reasons to cease this life,

she showed me only reasons to live.

She has made me feel that I do have worth.

When I think about how happy I would be

sharing my life with her,

I fall back to the reality that

I cannot share my life with her, and

the pain can be so terribly unbearable.

I wonder if she knows.

The enigma remains.

With her in my life, I have reason enough to live.

When I feel I will never have that opportunity,

I see only reasons to die.

I have lived in such pain for so long now,

I see no end.

I wonder, if I do go on,

will I see that dream come true, or

will it always be just a dream.

Does she have the same dream ?

There are so many lessons I would like to share with her,

so many of the lessons she has learned that

I would like her to share with me.

I wonder if she knows ?

SOFT GLOWING MOON 10/21/89 (A SONG)

I've walked down my road in the still of the night

The soft glowing moon and the diamond starlight

I've searched for the answer to the question of life

I've searched for a woman to become my wife

I've crossed the deserts and I've sailed the seas

Searching for someone to care for my needs

I've heard the wind dancing across empty skies

I've felt the tears as they flowed from my eyes

A man needs a woman to walk by his side

To put back the smile in his tired sad eyes

The love of a woman is warm and is sweet

A man needs a woman to make him complete

Often I've found myself sitting alone

On the bench in the park or the window at home

Hoping for someone to come my way

Hoping for someone to brighten my day

Sometimes I feel that I try too hard that

All I become is a world apart

All of my dreams seem to burn in the fires

From the love and the warmth that my heart desires

A man needs a woman to walk by his side

To put back the smile in his tired sad eyes

The love of a woman is warm and is sweet

A man needs a woman to make him complete

As the sun slowly brings on the night

I see in the sky a city of lights

Deep in my heart the emptiness grows but

Somehow my love continues to flow

Maybe some morning when the sun starts to rise

I will be able to open my eyes and

find myself in fields of wild clover

knowing that my life long journey is over

A man needs a woman to walk by his side

to put back the smile in his tired sad eyes

The love of a woman is warm and is sweet

a man needs a woman to make him complete

ONWARD THROUGH THE DARK

Tightly, grip the steely cold hands of loneliness.

Walking aimlessly in total darkness,

lost in the void of emptiness.

What do you hear when there is no sound?

What do you feel when the emotions you've

fought for so long are

finally surrendered to imprisonment

locked within the vault

so very deep within your heart?

Searching endlessly for a glimpse of light

a spark of hope.

Onward, slowly walking,

always wondering,

always praying.

I need to feel the gentle breeze,

once more,

touch my cheek,

cool my brow.

Onward, through the dark.

ONE STEP

I took one step down the path.

I heard the birds singing in the trees.

I could smell the flowers,

 sweet, soft,

  tickling my nose.

A cool and gentle breeze caressed my face.

I started thinking of old friends and

 happy times,

  the warmth of the sun, and

   the expectation of love.

I felt a peace within my heart,

 a light spirit within my being.

I started thinking about Country Lane.

It seems so long ago that

 I walked its welcoming trail,

  trees arched overhead,

   sunlight filtering down through the leaves.

It was magical, mystical,

 almost like a dream.

I started thinking about the waterfall.

I can still see the blazing blue sky,

 the radiant white clouds.

I can smell the leaves,

 so rich, so deep

  in color and scent.

The music from the falls still

 rings within my heart.

The birds and animals,

 so happy,

  so much at peace.

I remember a time,

 watching the sun set on the waves,

  golden, glowing.

   Children's laughter

    dancing on the wind,

     sailing through the air,

      lovers walking slowly

       holding hands.

Remembering, enjoying the memories,

 I put them away for the moment,

  took a second step, and

   continued on my way.

STARDUST

Stardust falling from the sky

Teardrops falling from my eyes

An empty hunger in my heart

Every night as we depart

A search for someone to fill my dreams

Someone to quiet the lonely screams

Someone to calm the thunderous storm

Someone to love the rose and thorn

Someone to take me as I am

Someone to sketch the diagram

Someone to hold me in their arms

Someone to capture me with their charms

Someone to walk barefoot through the heather

Someone to love me only forever

Stardust falling from the sky

Tears of happiness in my eyes

IF THESE THINGS I ONLY KNEW

A flower, glowing in the sunlight

stretching, reaching

to offer a smile to the earth.

I see the sun's golden rays

warming your heart.

A bird sitting in a tree

singing to all who listen.

Giving freely and

reveling in the happiness of knowing that

what is offered is

accepted with love.

A soft and gentle breeze

caresses my cheek,

cooling me, refreshing me.

A scent of peace upon wings,

bringing joy to my heart.

Stars sparkling like diamonds,

glistening with hope,

sharing love.

Rainbow lights

flickering like a candle flame.

Can you know my pain, my need?

Can you know my hunger for you?

Can you know the beauty I see

within your heart?

Can you know the emptiness inside

of not being with you,

those emotions I hide?

If I knew the words to say,

the things to do to make you stay,

I'd offer who I am to you,

if these things I only knew.

I WANTED TO TELL YOU 7/19/82 6:12 am

Sometimes, I think about all the times I wanted to tell you that

I cherish the time we spend together. That

when I am silent, my heart cries for you. That

I sit on my doorstep each day,

knowing that you will spend part of your morning with me. That

sometimes, I just want to embrace you, and

say thank you because you cared,

because you understood. That

I am happy when you are with me. That

I miss you when you are gone. That

I wish you could talk, and I could listen, but

time moves too quickly. That

even though I don't say it,

thank you for being you. That

you have made me feel there is trust. That

I wish I could say I love you, but

I don't know how.

TO BE AGAIN FREE

Morning comes,

blazing fire rising out of the waves.

Sea gulls dancing above the water.

I can feel the sand under me,

a sea of shifting solid form.

Salt sprays fill the air.

I remember days when

I would float on the sea,

water slapping the bow,

endless days with no sight of land,

sunlight then darkness,

over and over again.

Lines on charts guided me till

they became meaningless in their array.

Keep the heading, I'd keep repeating,

no one there to hear my heart beating

with hopes of drawing nearer to home

only to find myself once again gone.

I remember the feelings each time I would near

a point of land or pier.

feelings of triumph, of victory sweet,

knowing one day I would enter the deep.

For no one is victorious over the sea,

only the struggles to be again free.

COLORS IN THE LEAVES

I sat by the window today

watching squirrels play in the trees.

The sky was overcast bringing a

feeling of melancholy,

and emotions of

days gone by.

I thought about all the times

I would visit the forest

marveling at all the riches

lying in wait for those who would see.

There is a special something about

this time of year.

There is the crispness in the air,

a feeling of peace,

a feeling of love,

a hope for the future.

I love to see the many colored leaves.

It is such a different world

in the fall.

Leaves of red and gold and brown

adorn the trees as if

a child had drawn the world in crayons.

I remember a time when

I had watched a leaf fall from a tree.

I thought about how that leaf had been

born in the spring,

struggled for life all through summer,

finally to let go of the tree

knowing that after the transition it

would again become one with the earth.

I could feel the faith and the hope that

leaf must have felt.

I could feel the sacrifice it had made.

It was so nice to be so close to the earth.

I would always feel an excitement from

watching rabbits hopping through fallen leaves.

They would stop, scratch around for some morsel of food, then

on they would go again.

They were so happy,

so peaceful in their lives.

Birds were busy preparing their nests for the

coming snow.

They would sing songs of life for all to hear.

You could hear music as the wind would

dance through the trees.

Whistling as it moved from limb to limb.

I could feel compassion as the breezes would

caress each tree, each leaf,

as if it were saying,

"Be calm, my friend, for

lonely times come, but

soon will be the rebirth of spring."

Such comfort I'd feel.

Autumn is so much like times in our life when

we would feel lonely, or sad.

We all have that friend who reminds us of

a coming rebirth.

Always keep hope and faith close to your heart.

COURAGE UNBENDING

Onward, march the brave and the willing,

into the unknown,

into the murky swamps of

pasts and futures.

Knowing not if to fight,

only knowing the anticipation,

the waiting.

Such faith, such loyalty

to go to arms for freedom

and love of life.

Why, can they answer,

is death sometimes required

to maintain life?

Why, at times, must bondage to a cause

be required to bring freedom?

To march into battle with

head held high,

emotions stirring in the heart,

confusions mixing within the mind,

marching onward,

never faltering,

courage unbending,

knowing the price of honor.

To these soldiers of freedom

I send my strength,

my loyalty,

my faith in their cause.

My respect shall follow them

to whatever place in the mind and heart

they shall journey.

MEMORY WELL

Many times I find myself

walking around inside my mind,

remembering old friends, so long ago seen,

happy times, and

hopeful dreams.

I can see times when I would

walk through the forest

marveling at many of God's creations.

I could see squirrels hiding acorns, and

birds building nests,

flowers so tiny and spiders in webs.

Dew sparkled like diamonds

on the face of the leaves,

the scent of honeysuckle floating on the breeze.

I'd sit for hours listening to

the concert of the forest world,

their songs and their tunes.

such peace they would bring me

in times of my stress.

The beauty of nature,

the grace of egrets

gliding above their image below

on water like a mirror,

they'd come and they'd go.

Although, no longer do I frequent their realm,

I can always draw their happiness from

my precious, memory well.

OLD FRIEND

Well, old friend, I guess neither of us thought this day would ever come.

I was just thinking about how we met, and all the good times and the not

so good times that we shared. It was like our meeting was some kind of

strange twist of fate. I can still see it like it was yesterday.

I remember seeing him leaning against the wall, then he just started

falling over. I was frozen in disbelief as I watched him tumble. It

seemed like he fell forever. Then when he finally landed the sound was

something I'll never forget. I can remember jumping up and running over to

him. It was a nightmare, pieces here, and there. I was so hurt. I felt

so very alone. It was over.

Well, I guess if it wasn't for the accident, we'd never have met. I

can still see the day I went downtown. I remember the emotions I felt

when I saw you standing in the music shop. I could feel my eyes light

up as I just stood there and looked at you. I remember the first time

I held you in my arms. You felt like such a lady to me. I can still

feel the happiness I felt then.

We've had so many good times together. It was so nice going to the park

with you. Everyone seemed to like you the moment they saw you. And, then,

when you started to sing, it was like everyone had to sing along with you.

We met so many nice people there. I remember how you used to like going

to the dam. We'd go out early in the morning before the sun rose.

There was that favorite picnic table we used to sit at down by the water.

We never caught any fish, but we had such good times just sitting there

singing and playing music. That old man who couldn't talk would come down

every Sunday. He sits, and reads his paper. Then after a couple hours

his friend would meet him and they would sit for a while just enjoying

the peace and the solitude.

I remember the time we went to that funeral. People looked at us kind of

strangely when we first went in. There I was in my long hair, beard, and

three piece suit. I was dressed to the hilt. And, there you were in all

your shining beauty. When you started singing so softly and so sweetly

they seemed to feel more comfortable with us being there.

I sit here and I think back on all the songs we've written together. I

remember all the times you were here for me. There were times when I was

happy and you were happy with me. There were times when I was sad and

you consoled me. There were times when I was lonely and you sang to me.

You always let me be myself. You always let me express myself. You never

laughed at me.

I remember the concert we played at. I can see us up on the stage. There

was that elderly lady standing in the back of the crowd. When we were

getting ready to take a break that lady starting heading up toward the

stage. It touched me that she would come all that way through that crowd just to get a closer look at you. I felt so proud.

I guess you're going to stay with Max for a while now. It hurts me that you're leaving. I'm going to miss you. I hoped that we would never have to be apart, but I guess somewhere deep in my heart, I always knew this day would come. I just want you to know how much I care for you, and that no matter what happens to me in this lifetime, I'll never have another like you. You are truly a one of a kind. You have been a true friend to me. You were always there for me, but never expected anything from me. I will never have another guitar like you.

THE VOICE IN THE WIND

So many lives have come and gone

like seasons in the winds

sometimes it's hard to picture

where this timeless walk begins

so long ago I lost you on a

cold and moonless night

we need to meet just once again

before the coming light

It seems we've searched forever

looking for that love we lost

we've seen many battles and

we've fought for many a cause

but those lives were just a passing mist

while we traveled onward still

with memories of a spirit kiss

and an undying spirit will

You sat before me on the lawn

your robe purple trimmed with gold

behind you lay the ruins of

a city long grown cold

a bowl you carved of aging wood

you placed gently on the ground

music floated on the wind like

soft and graceful sounds

I can see a picture in my mind

of a lonely seaport town

I looked up to the window

to see you looking down

a feeling touched my very soul

as if we had known sometime

we had been together in

a past forgotten life

Another time I saw you as

they brought me from the field

wounded by the musket

of the man I tried to kill

brother against brother and

father against son

the battle of the blue and gray

was my setting sun

Onward through the pages

from life to life we roam

searching for each other so that

we finally may travel home

just out of reach from each other's arms

we seem to always be

locked inside unrequited love

we have to find the key

Hold on to faith, surrender not

for one day we shall meet

the emptiness of this life without you

shall not my love deplete

Though our paths may parallel this life

hold dearly to this thought

I shall search through eternity

until our paths shall cross

Chorus :

We cry into the emptiness and

the darkness in the land

we walk forever reaching

for that warm and gentle hand

how long must we journey

before we find the love we seek

though our hearts may tire

they never will grow weak

WILL I ALWAYS WONDER 7/31/90

Standing on the pier

I notice so very many different things.

I can smell the wooden planks

scented with salt and age

the fragrance taking me back

to long ago days.

I hear the music of waves

gently slapping against the rocks

a lullaby to sleeping gulls.

I look out over the water as

the reflection of the moon

ripples through memories

I sometimes remember.

My mind slowly fading from the reality

going back

back in time to a place in my heart.

Remembering the long nights without you

the time when I could see the

sparkle of diamonds in your eyes.

When I could smell the sweet

perfume of your spirit.

When I could feel the

brush of your hair

like silk.

When I could hear your voice

like a song on the gentle breeze

refreshing to my being.

When I could feel your warmth

your tenderness

your caring.

When I could reach out to you

stroke your cheek

see your gentle smile.

How I long for you to be here with me.

I needed you then.

I need you now.

So many times I have

felt in my heart the

first moment you held me in your arms.

Will I ever know how this would feel

in reality or

will I always wonder?

TIME WAITS FOR NONE

So many memories, so little time.

We spent many, many hours

chatting, talking, listening,

just knowing the other was within reach.

But, oh, time passes so quickly.

There were times when we laughed,

times when we hurt,

times when we cried.

Odd how time softens some emotions, but

sharpens others.

How time can seem like forever, and then

seem to pass in the blink of an eye.

So long we've planned,

so long we've dreamed,

so often we've played this movie in our minds.

The time is finally come.

The anxiety of this moment,

our first meeting,

the excitement, the thrill, the

unsureness of the outcome.

Footsteps as she comes down the hall,

her breath coming in short, excited gasps as

she opens the door and steps through.

Emotions running high, sounds of the world

fading into the background as the nurse turns and says,

"I'm sorry, he's gone, but he left you this message..."

"My dearest friend,

My heart aches to know that

I am no longer here, that

you cannot hear me speak these words to you.

Though we never met in this world,

I feel our spirits have already joined as one.

You gave me such treasures of kindness,

of trust,

of faith,

of caring,

of knowing that I was cared for.

Your gifts I shall carry with me,

in my heart,

in my spirit,

in my eternity.

Dreams are wonderful.

Do not fear to dream.

Cherish your dreams, but

do not let your dreams become your life.

Allow your life to reach your dreams.

For it is an eternal truth,

time waits for none."

I WATCHED YOUR SUNSET

I sat, contemplating days and memories and

I watched your sunset.

As the sun slowly reached for the horizon

I saw the soft, pastel pink of your lips,

a soft and reassuring gentle kiss to the end of the day.

As the rays glistened against the rich, green leaves

I saw the emeralds and diamonds of your eyes.

Waves of grain gently rolled in the evening breeze like the

silkiness of your angelic hair.

As the soft, glowing moon

gracefully climbed to the top of the sky

I saw the velvety, creamy caress of your cheek.

Birds quietly chirping,

wishing a peaceful evening to the earth

rang with the sweetness of your voice.

I watched your sunset tonight and it

brought a peace to my heart

knowing that you are a part of my being.

I walked out into the

 still, night air

  the sky mottled with clouds

   drifting slowly

    aimlessly

     like thoughts in a pondering mind

moonlight filtering down like

 gently settling dust

  no hurry

   no fears

    possessing only a need to be

calm fills my being

 solitude finds a home

  peace in knowing that

   all is well

THUNDER IN THE DISTANCE

I listened to the lullaby of far off thunder

the hypnotic tapping of raindrops against the window and

I thought about you.

There you were in your own world

slowly and softly rocking in your bentwood

lost within the pages of someone else's words.

Fire passively lolling in the fireplace, it's

soft glow bears a warmth to the room,

It's golden shadows dancing upon the walls.

You were the picture of peace, the

picture of contentment, the

picture of harmony with all.

I watched as the dancing flames cast

diamonds of twinkling light

into your eyes.

My heart longed to reach out to you, but

I chose to wait, to not disturb your gift to me of

the serenity of knowing that someone cares.

EVERY DROP OF RAIN

With every drop of rain

I feel the pain of

words never spoken

hearts silently broken

like the shadows in the

darkness of my mind.

A thousand times I've

watched you walk away.

You couldn't stay.

I always knew you'd leave.

My tears mingle with

the silence of the rain

the echoes of the pain

within my soul.

I WONDER WHY

As I go through life, I sometimes wonder why.

Why do I go on, what am I searching for.

Have I found it or do I believe, deep inside, that

I never will.

I paid my dues, but why am I still paying, and for what.

I feel like I'm walking in circles going nowhere.

Time really has no meaning for me anymore.

I come, I go, I seek, but

I never seem to find.

When I feel like I've found happiness, it is like

a picture on the wall.

I can look at it, but I still cannot live in its reality.

It is like dreams.

Dreams are all I have, but

where is the reality.

What is my reality.

Where do I go from here.

Why should I go on.

STRENGTH OF MY FATHER

I thought that I cried because I was afraid for him.

I realized I cried because of my own fears...

my fears of weakness...

my fears of losing a hard fought battle.

I saw him march onward with his head held high.

He had the spirit of a warrior.

He was not afraid.

I stopped crying.

I held my head high

knowing that his courage is what

makes him a survivor...

a conqueror.

Now, I am able to be strong for him.

FINAL BATTLE WINNER TAKE ALL

I have fought the good fight. I still fight the good fight.

When my time comes I will not go quietly into that night, but

I will fight and dig for every inch of ground I can attain.

Because I will not concede, because I will not quit

I am a winner. I am a champion for my cause.

When my eyes close to darkness for the last time

I will shout...I will cheer.

I will raise my arms in victory because

I AM the winner...winner take all!

IF TOMORROW

If tomorrow I should be

only a memory please remember

I have loved and

cherished and shall

miss each and

every one of you.

Know that my journey has

called me to move onward to

places yet unknown

places I've not yet seen

memories I've not yet made.

Although I shall not return

perhaps I shall live on

within your heart.

Made in the USA
Columbia, SC
09 April 2018